Mary Pipes has worked in journalism and public relations. *Understanding Abortion* was her first book. Since its first publication she has trained as a person-centred counsellor. She has worked as a therapist in the UK and in Pakistan, and now lives and works in Sri Lanka.

Women's Health is an independent information and resource centre for women on health matters. They offer an enquiry service by phone and post; publications on various issues; and a quarterly newsletter. They also have a large reference library of books, articles, news clippings and pamphlets.

MARY PIPES
WITH
WOMEN'S HEALTH

Understanding
Abortion

NEW EDITION,
FULLY REVISED AND UPDATED

To all the women who wrote this book
and to Geraldine

First published by The Women's Press Ltd, 1986
A member of the Namara Group
34 Great Sutton Street, London EC1V 0DX

New edition 1998

British Library Cataloguing-in-Publication Data
A catalogue record for this book is available from the British Library.

ISBN 0 7043 4480 7

Typeset in Sabon 11/12pt by FSH Ltd, London
Printed and bound in Great Britain by Cox & Wyman Ltd,
Reading, Berkshire

Contents

Preface to the Second Edition

In the twelve years since the first edition of this book, the context of abortion has changed dramatically for women in the UK. The rise of specialised abortion clinics in which women are cared for by committed and experienced staff has meant that the experience of abortion for most women is now very different. Improved over-the-counter pregnancy tests allow earlier detection of unwanted pregnancies, reflected in a corresponding shift to earlier abortions. Early medical abortion and walk-in daycare procedures have helped to normalise abortion and have given women wider choice and more control. Public support for abortion on demand has grown, with surveys repeatedly showing a sizeable majority who agree that abortion should be legally available for those who want it.

One thing that hasn't changed is the demand for information on abortion. Requests for abortion leaflets from schoolchildren and older students are among the most common enquiries Women's Health receive. The UK has the highest pregnancy rate among 15–19-year-olds in western Europe. Sex education is inadequate, contraception fails, and tragically, women are still raped and coerced into sex. The confusion over the health risks of third generation contraceptive pills at the end of 1995 resulted in an increase in the number of unwanted pregnancies, reversing a long-term downward trend in the number of abortions. Despite the changes in abortion services, books like *Understanding Abortion* are still vital.

Women's Health
May 1998

Acknowledgements

For Information

Many, many thanks to the following organisations for all the information they made available and for the assistance with the circulation of questionnaires which some of them gave: British Pregnancy Advisory Service, Brook Advisory Centres, Marie Stopes International, Dublin Well Woman Centre, Abortion Law Reform Association, Birth Control Campaign and Birth Control Trust, National Abortion Campaign.

For Permission to Reprint

The authors gratefully acknowledge permission from the following to reprint material in this book: Policy Studies Institute for quotations from Isobel Allen, *Abortion, Sterilisation and Family Planning* (1981); The DHSS and Royal College of Obstetricians and Gynaecologists for information contained in *Late Abortions in England and Wales (1984); Family Planning Perspectives* for quotations from *Repeat Abortion: Is it a Problem?*, Vol.16, No.2 (March/April 1984); Open Line Counselling for its survey of its first 202 clients.

Help, Advice and Support

Without the editorial planning, suggestions, word-processing skills, hours of proof-reading and even more hours of typing and the constant support and encouragement which was given freely by my friend Andy M. this book would never have taken shape. I would also like to thank Joan Maizells for her advice on the questionnaires, Kate Meadows and Collette Hagely for listening, Joanne Litson for supportive letters from Australia, Robin Sibley for telling me I should write it, and David Kwo for gathering information in New York.

In addition, Women's Health would like to thank the Abortion Providers Federation of Australia; the Birth Control Trust; British Pregnancy Advisory Services; Dublin Well Woman Centre; the Irish Women's Abortion Support Group; the Family Planning Association.

To the Women Who Wrote This Book

This book is based on the personal accounts of 30 women who hoped that, by sharing their experiences, it would be possible for others to understand more fully the practical and complex emotional reality of abortion. There is nothing I can write which can express the depth of my thanks or my enormous debt to these women, for they have made it possible to understand.

Introduction

Every woman's experience of abortion is different

For some of us the decision to terminate our pregnancy is an easy one, unaccompanied by doubts about the rightness of our decision or post-abortion feelings of guilt and remorse. In fact, many women feel an enormous sense of relief when the whole process is over. However, for others it is a painful and traumatic period of our lives when we are wracked by the ambivalence of our emotions, on the one hand wanting to have a baby, on the other, knowing it is not the right time for us to do so. We sometimes feel we have committed murder, we question our sexuality, our relationship with our lovers, children and parents and find ourselves confronting our own deep beliefs and needs. We feel angry and sorrowful before and after our experience, yet we can also emerge from it with a greater understanding of ourselves.

The following accounts, of how two women reacted to the experience of having an abortion, have been printed in full in order to show the whole experience before looking in detail at the different stages of each woman's journey. The first was taken from a taped interview and the second from the woman's own full-length account and the questionnaire she filled in. Here, as elsewhere in the book, square brackets have been used to indicate where I have inserted my own words to link passages.

Helen:

I think I had my abortion in the spring or autumn of 1973, I remember the weather rather than the date. I was nineteen. It was a one-night stand who I had known for some time. We had a party at our house and we ended up in bed together which I suppose we had always wanted to do, out of curiosity rather than anything more serious. I never told him I was pregnant because it was a one-night stand.

I was very disorganised with contraception at that time, I used a combination of the rhythm method, withdrawal and prayer, which on this occasion failed me ...

I had always been one of those people who theoretically thought abortion was all right, but would never do it myself. But as soon as I realised I was pregnant, I knew that I wanted an abortion. There was never any question about it. I sort of knew better where to begin looking than a lot of the women I knew at the time and phoned a helpline because I was convinced it would be terribly difficult to get one. I phoned them to say, 'Look, I really, really want an abortion and what do I have to say to these people to persuade them to give me one?' And they said, 'Oh, you just phone PAS (Pregnancy Advisory Service)! Don't worry, just relax, they'll talk to you about it.' And that was the first sign I had that I wasn't going to have to go through enormous hoops of pretending that I'd have a mental breakdown if I was pregnant, which I knew perfectly well I wouldn't do, but which I was convinced I would have to do.

[When I went] along to the PAS the woman who interviewed me assumed that I had absolutely decided to have an abortion and that was interesting because again I thought that I was going to have to pretend that I needed her help to make up my mind, which I didn't at all.

I didn't tell anyone about it apart from my sister. It's difficult to say why, one of the reasons is the more people you tell, the more messy things get . . .

I remember the visit to the clinic vividly. You had to get a Tube to about as far out as it would go and then there was a bus and you had to get off about four stops on, and there I was anxiously looking at my piece of paper and peering out to see if was the right stop and this lovely little old woman said to me, 'It's all right dear, I'll tell you when to get off.' Obviously every morning there was a little trail of nineteen-year-olds getting the bus from the station to the clinic! . . .

It was all quite swift and I really can't remember much about it. My sister tells me I was upset about something one of the nurses said, but I can't remember it so I can't have been very upset. I remember them being brisk and it was a bit like a production line, but I think if I was a nurse it would be a bit like that.

It was under general anaesthetic . . . and I don't know what they did to me: I didn't ask and they didn't offer . . .

I don't remember it as a painful experience at all. I remember my pubic hairs growing back and the itchiness of that better than any pain or cramps.

Afterwards there were bits of it I thought about but they were more to do with the other people [who were having abortions] than with me. I just parked it there among experiences, as I think one does, not as something to be mulled over . . . I never regretted what I'd done.

Katie:

The second conception took place just prior to midwifery finals, the pregnancy finally being 'tested' in the very north of Scotland, amidst pending results from exams, results of a place on a subsequent Health Visitors' course and a system which took eight weeks to tell me that I was pregnant, by which time I had returned to the South East! En route, I confirmed my worst fears using *Discover 2* [a pregnancy testing kit]. (I ought to have shares, I've bought so many!)

We had both just about come to terms with what the pregnancy was going to do to my career, to our finances, which were not good, and our lives as individuals when at thirteen weeks I bled extremely heavily and called out the GP [not my usual GP]. I couldn't show him what I had passed as there was so much. I had naturally sat on the loo and someone in the house had cleared up the mess and flushed it away. The GP never took his hands out of his pockets and said, 'Did I think it was complete?' And that was it!

After he had paid his brief visit I did my own vaginal examination to reassure myself that my cervix was closed. It was, and the bleeding had stopped.

The next morning our brief tears convinced me that we had begun to adjust [to the idea of having a baby together]. I did a further pregnancy test which was positive but was reassured by the surgery that it took a while for pregnancy hormones to return to a normal level. I would have liked a scan to convince me, but the haemorrhage was so large and I felt large clots, etc. being passed so I left it at that.

Finally I regained my college place and sponsorship [given up at the time of pregnancy] and began the 65 miles each way to college. The very arduous health visitor training plus 130 miles daily in winter was made even more exhausting by my increasing 'oedema' [excessive water retention], breast tabdominal [tenderness] and backache.

During this time my usual GP was consulted and over a period of three months I was prescribed antibiotics, diuretics and laxatives for the 'oedema', progesterone for the 'obvious hormonal imbalance', *Brufen* for the backache, *Migraleve* for the headaches and finally valium to sleep (I was getting edgy at feeling so ill and the GP's idea that I had a pituitary tumour!) and *Bromocriptine* for the obvious hyper-prolactinaemia [tumour-causing lactation].

After several weeks of this and feeling my body belonged to the NHS, it occurred to us both that the amenorrhoea [no menstrual periods], bloatedness, backache, emaciation but small weight gain could mean only one thing, and that thing was confirmed by definite foetal movements. The next day I did another pregnancy test and presented the positive, 23-weeks' result to my disbelieving GP.

After all the six months' ups and downs, the course and most of the drugs, some teratogenic [drugs absorbed into the placenta which could deform the foetus], all undesirable, we knew there was no choice. After three days of sheer hell I was admitted for a hysterotomy [similar to delivery by Caesarean section] . . .

The night before I went into hospital, I had no sleep. I felt a definite dichotomy between what my logic told me was in the long term the *right* thing to do, and my body and female psyche knowing that this was an unnatural and murderous act which totally conflicted with my every philosophy, that of vegetarian, nature lover and nurse. I thought of all the young animals I had tended and cherished, of nature's wonders of the creation of life and growth, of all the babies I had delivered and the early terminations and later ones too that I had assisted as a professional. I was confused, torn and literally *in pieces* but my resolve held it all together – just about.

At 24 weeks pregnant I killed a baby girl, became an ardent feminist and never trusted orthodox medicine again.

Abortion is indisputably a political issue, both in the sense of the arena of party politics and as a subject with which the women's movement world wide is concerned. Because I believe that it is women who should decide when and with whom they want children, and not political, religious or medical institutions, I could not write this book without placing it in a feminist and therefore political perspective. At the same time, however, abortion is experienced in a deeply personal, and emotional, way.

The more involved I became with the women who offered to help with this book, the more I realised that I could not make any easy generalisations about their experiences. To say that some of us suffer because the patriarchal society within which we live often condemns abortion and oppresses the right of women to control their own bodies, is true, but it is not the whole story. It does not explain why, for instance, one women who approves of abortion, who is supported by her friends and lover throughout the whole experience and who receives sympathetic and non-judgemental treatment from the medical profession should feel that she has killed a child, while another woman who is largely disapproving of abortion and who receives indifferent treatment should find the decision easy to make and feel only relief afterwards.

While nearly all of us can be neatly classified into one or more groups, by race, colour, age, class, religion, sexuality, and are often influenced by the dominant views which that group holds on abortion when choosing to have one ourselves, we are also individuals. The experiences we have as children, teenagers and adults, the ideas and people with whom we come into contact all play a part in our development and influence the way we feel about ourselves. Consequently the way each of us experiences, interprets and copes with the pressures and support both from outside and from within ourselves at the time of our abortion will be unique.

When writing this book, therefore, I have tried to avoid making any generalisations about the way in which women react to and cope with the experience of having an abortion. Instead I have let the women's accounts speak for themselves in the belief that the broader picture is the more accurate one.

In deciding to do this I faced my own dilemma: a conflict between my political belief that as women we must be free to choose to terminate our unwanted pregnancies, and my promise to be totally truthful to all the women who had entrusted me and The Women's Press with their experiences. I was worried that by exploring the most painful accounts, I would be providing the anti-abortionists with the emotive and 'sensational' material used in their campaigns to restrict the provision of safe, legal terminations – campaigns whose success would, at best, give women no choice but to organise their own illegal abortions and, at worst, result in a return to back-street practitioners. I was also concerned that these same experiences might make it more difficult for some women to make their own decisions about whether or not to terminate their own pregnancies.

Ultimately the resolution was provided by all the women who contributed to the handbook. For, as a result of their experiences and regardless of their views on abortion before choosing to have one themselves, not one woman advocated any restrictive change in the law in Britain. Many felt even more strongly that abortion should be available, free of charge, to all those who request it. The exclusion of these accounts would in essence have been as dishonest as any of the material which the anti-abortion organisations circulate since it would have been a denial of what, for some women, is the reality of abortion.

Furthermore the accounts revealed that, contrary to the anti-abortionists' claims, an abortion is not just a negative experience.

By facing the issues that terminating a pregnancy can raise, many women have learned more about themselves. This in turn has led them to make changes so that their lives become an expression of who they truly are, rather than an expression of who they think they should be.

1
Discovering You Are Pregnant

> I mean, it's the one thing you'd always been told, right
> from being a kid: 'Don't get pregnant. Don't get
> pregnant. If you can't be good, be careful.' And all
> those feelings were there.   *Sandra*

The realisation that you may be pregnant unleashes a
complex and sometimes unexpected mix of emotions. Even
women who consciously desire and plan their pregnancy
may be taken by surprise by feelings of fear, resentment and
ambivalence. If the pregnancy is unplanned, some women
still feel pleased to discover that they are fertile, even if they
plan to have an abortion. There is little social acknow-
ledgement of these complicated and deeply personal
feelings, no public discussion of how women really feel
about pregnancy and abortion. This is because there is a
strong assumption, even in our modern society, that a
woman's most important role is to be a mother. Connected
with this is another powerful social belief: that, in some
way, all pregnancies are not just the business of the

pregnant woman, but are owned by the society in which she lives and the man with whom she has had sex. A woman who is suddenly faced with the possibility of pregnancy must deal with these strong but unspoken social pressures as she tries to sort out her own feelings.

How unwanted pregnancies occur

Another implicit social assumption is that women are to blame for unwanted pregnancies. Although some people believe that many young girls become pregnant intentionally to escape from their parents, to receive benefits and so on, most pregnancies in teenagers are accidental.[1] Yet many people still refuse to recognise that contraception can fail or may not be available, that women and girls may be coerced and bullied into unprotected sex, that some women may not understand how their bodies work, or may have reasons to believe that they cannot get pregnant.

Not using contraception

A study of women requesting abortion in Britain found that three out of ten did not use contraception at the time they became pregnant.[2] The popular belief that every woman knows how to control her fertility and can therefore prevent herself from becoming pregnant is simply not true. Some young women may have received little or no education either on sex or contraception, and may not understand how their bodies work or even how sexual activity with a man can lead to pregnancy. A client profile carried out by Open Line, Dublin revealed that although 57.2 per cent of the women it had counselled had some experience of contraception, 75.6 per cent had not used any method at the time of conception, and a further 36.3 per cent had never used any method. Open Line concluded that, 'contraception, and appropriate education and information, is not sufficiently available to the people who need it.'[3] Although carried out in 1983, unfortunately this survey's findings are still relevant today; more recent studies show that knowledge about contraception continues to be inadequate.[4]

Nor was it the young who suffered most from the lack of information. Of the 202 women Open Line saw in its first year, only 15.8 percent were between 16 and 19, indicating that misinformation can persist for many years if we live in repressive communities. One Irish woman who conceived when she was 25 explained:

I was living in Paris prior to Cyprus and had a few sexual encounters without protection, so a friend passed me a packet of the pill which I used in a haphazard fashion, i.e. forgetting for a day or two then remembering. When I eventually went to Cyprus I don't think I had continued at all with the pill. I realise now it was a lack of recognition of my sexuality and the consequences of sexual relations – unprotected – a distinct gap in my education.   *Marie*

In Britain, sex education has become fairly widespread over the last 25 years, but there has not been a corresponding fall in the number of unwanted pregnancies ending in abortion. Official figures reveal that in England and Wales in 1977 there were 15.13 abortions per 1000 women aged 15–19; in 1995 the rate had risen to 21.7.[5]

But for most women in Britain and even in Ireland where attitudes towards contraception have relaxed in recent years, the reasons for not using contraception are more complicated than simply not knowing that it exists. Young women in particular may not feel empowered to use contraception; or they may know about contraception but use it inconsistently or incorrectly.

Young women may have low self-esteem, leading them to go along with their boyfriends' demands for sex despite fear of pregnancy. They may not plan to have sex, and therefore may not have any contraception, but find themselves in situations which they feel are out of their control. A sense of personal worth and confidence is important if girls are to make decisions for themselves and not simply in response to pressure from boys, their peers or popular culture.

Many women who use contraception do not understand how to use it properly. Several studies have shown that up to half of women using the pill are not aware that stomach upsets can reduce its effectiveness, and in one study 11 per cent of pill users did not know that they had to take the pill every day.[6] A further problem is poor knowledge of postcoital or emergency contraception, commonly but incorrectly called the 'morning-after pill'. The majority of women do not realise that this form of contraception can be used up to three days after unprotected intercourse.

The amount of knowledge about contraception that a woman has, and her ability to act on that knowledge, is strongly affected by her cultural background and the society in which she lives. In Britain, white women score highest on tests of contraception knowledge and black women score significantly less, regardless of their level of education, indicating unequal access to appropriate contraception information and services.

There are still those who do not receive information or who do not understand what they are told and are too nervous to enquire further. These women are most at risk of believing popular myths such as, 'You can't get pregnant the first time'; 'You're not fertile till you get older', and that 'pulling out in time' will prevent conception.

Lack of availability

Even if we know about contraception, we may not have access to any. One study indicates that fewer than one in five Irish women seeking abortion in England felt that they

had access to contraception.[7] Until quite recently, many
GPs in Ireland would only prescribe contraception to
married women living with their husbands, while some
refused to prescribe contraception regardless of a woman's
marital circumstances. Now, however, about two-thirds of
GPs claim to offer family planning services,[8] and there are
also family planning centres in the cities, including three in
Dublin. But because the GP is also the family doctor,
separate family planning centres are crucial; their
contraception advice is felt to be much more confidential
than that offered by GPs. Many young unmarried women
who use these centres specifically mention a dread of their
family finding out that they are on the pill.[9] For women in
rural areas of Ireland contraception remains difficult to
obtain, although since 1993 the law has allowed the sale of
condoms to those over the age of 17, and through outlets
other than pharmacies.

Although contraception is seemingly more easily
available in Britain, young women often feel shy and
unwilling to ask their GP about it. Almost half of 16–19-
year-olds and three-quarters of under 16s in a 1991
survey said they feared their GP would not preserve
confidentiality if they requested contraception.[10] Many
do not realise that they can register with another GP for
contraception services if they wish.

There is still some confusion in many people's minds
about whether doctors can prescribe contraception to
girls under 16 without their parents' consent. This is
because of a Court of Appeal ruling in 1984 which
banned doctors from doing so. This ruling is known as
the Gillick ruling after Victoria Gillick, who campaigned
for the court decision. Mrs Gillick, a mother of ten and
a Roman Catholic, did not wish her daughters to be
given advice about contraception or abortion without
her consent. In 1985 the House of Lords reversed the ban
and established the current legal position in England and

Wales. This is that people under 16 are legally able to consent on their own behalf to any surgical, medical or dental procedure or treatment if, in the doctor's opinion, they are capable of understanding the nature and possible consequences of the procedure. Scottish law is equivalent. In relation to contraception services, when consulted by people under 16, doctors are required to:

- consider whether the patient understands the potential risks and benefits of the treatment and the advice given
- discuss the value of parental support and encourage young people to inform their parents of the consultation, exploring the reasons if the patient is unwilling to do so. Even though the doctor is legally obliged to discuss the value of parental support, he or she must observe confidentiality
- take into account whether the person is likely to have sexual intercourse without contraception
- assess whether the patient's physical and mental health, or both, are likely to suffer if they do not receive contraception advice or supplies
- consider whether the patient's best interests would require the provision of contraception advice or methods without parental consent

If the doctor has reason to believe that the person seeking advice is being exploited or abused, the law requires him or her to provide counselling with a view to preparing the patient to agree, when ready, to confidentiality being relaxed. In a situation of risk, the doctor may have to tell the patient that confidentiality cannot be preserved. Even in these extreme situations the doctor is advised to discuss disclosure with the patient first.

Despite the fact that this guidance has made it possible for many young women under 16 to obtain advice or supplies of contraception, some teenagers are unaware of it while others are confused about the legality of sexual intercourse for women under 16. The Sexual Offences Act 1956, which relates to the age of consent to sexual intercourse, is somewhat complex. Although the Act states that it is an absolute offence for a man to have intercourse with a girl under 13 years, it is less clear about those over 13. It states that it is an offence for a man to have intercourse with a girl aged between 13 and 16 years *unless* the man is under 14 (in which case he is not liable for prosecution), *or* if he is under 24 and has not previously been charged with an offence of this kind and believes the girl to be over 16, or if he believes himself to be validly married to the girl (although this is not so). A women under 16 does not commit an offence by having intercourse. This law applies to England and Wales and a similar law, the Sexual Offences (Scotland) Act 1956, applies to Scotland.

Not surprisingly many teenagers don't understand the law, believing that both partners are committing a crime by having intercourse. Young women under 16 are therefore inhibited from going to a doctor or clinic to ask for contraception, because they do not want to admit what they believe is a criminal act to someone in authority. In some instances their beliefs are substantiated by those doctors who do not wish to prescribe birth control because they believe they would thereby be aiding and abetting an offence.

Even for a woman over 16 the fear that her GP will tell her parents may be so strong that she decides not to seek help. If she does not know of the existence of or how to find the address of a Brook Advisory Centre or a sympathetic family planning clinic, she may decide to risk unprotected intercourse, particularly when both she and her boyfriend are too embarrassed to buy condoms or are unsure of how to use them.

The extent to which a young woman feels she can seek help from the available sources will also be determined by her relationship with her parents. A girl whose parents are relaxed about her sexuality, knowledgeable about contraception, and will discuss this with her, is far more likely to ask for contraceptive advice than one who has parents who openly disapprove. Sometimes the fear of parents discovering any contraception that a young woman might have is so strong that it dissuades her from attempting to use birth control. Women brought up by cultural norms that require them to be a virgin at the time of their marriage will be especially vulnerable to this fear, as it is not unusual in some cultures for parents to disown their daughters if they discover they have had sexual relations.

Lack of advocacy or interpreter services is a major barrier to access to contraceptive services for women who do not speak English. These women rely on the help of health advocates who act as interpreters and provide health information and advice. But Health Authorities provide health advocates for only a fraction of GP practices, and for only two or three sessions a week. Women either face delays in seeing their doctor, or have to use family members, often their husbands and young children, as interpreters. This creates obvious difficulties for women wanting contraceptive advice, especially if they choose not to discuss it with their husbands, or if they are unmarried.

Choosing not to use contraception

> When I told my friends I was pregnant, they were very sympathetic, but I think one or two of them were a bit amazed that I wasn't using any birth control.   *Liz*

The method of birth control which has done more to create the belief that we don't need to become pregnant unless we choose to is the pill. Although the pill has freed many women from pain and heavy bleeding, it doesn't suit everyone.

My knowledge of birth control then and now is high, but I feel my decision to discontinue oral contraceptives was partly due to a documentary I had seen on television which (I hope I recall accurately) stated that there were only twelve hours in each month when fertilisation could occur. I remember thinking that it hardly seemed worth taking the pill for a whole 21 days for the sake of twelve hours.   *Vanessa*

Unwanted pregnancies rose significantly in Britain following the pill scare of October 1995. The Committee on Safety in Medicine announced that women taking the so-called 'third generation' oral contraceptive pill (those containing desogestrel, gestodene and norgestimate) faced a doubled risk of blood clots in the veins compared with women who took other forms of contraceptive pill. The impact was immediate. A survey of third-generation pill users by British Pregnancy Advisory Services (BPAS) in April 1996 showed that 41 per cent of these women stopped taking the pill immediately and a further 20 per cent did not finish their current course of pills.[11] An estimated 300,000 women stopped taking the pill or switched contraception. The result was an increase of 6.3 per cent in the number of abortions in the subsequent three months, reversing a trend of falling abortion figures which had been evident since 1991.[12] Much of the anxiety and confusion about third-generation pills arose because the original announcement was based on unpublished results. Doctors were unaware that the announcement was imminent, and they could not turn to the medical journals, read the studies for themselves, and advise their patients. When the studies were eventually published in January 1996[13] the conclusion was confirmed but put into context. The BPAS report says that women should have been told that the risk of blood clots is far less than the risks associated with unwanted pregnancy. Doctors also point out that the greatest risk to health comes from smoking while on the pill, rather than the type of pill being used.

Those women who reject the pill can find it difficult to choose an alternative they feel happy with, particularly if they have an unsympathetic doctor. Ideally a doctor should assist us in exploring the other methods that are available, ask us how we would feel about using them, and make sure that we and our partners are fully aware of the commitment they involve. Some doctors, however, do not encourage us to make our own choices about contraception. Instead they prescribe what they believe we would be happy with. When we come to use the method, particularly if our first experiences are unhappy ones, our lack of participation in the choice is not likely to encourage us to persevere.

For some women finding a method of contraception with which they feel happy and confident can be a nightmare.

> At the time I conceived I was like a walking encyclopaedia of contraceptive knowledge. After trying countless brands of pills, high dosage, low dosage, mini; a *Copper 7* [an IUD]; a diaphragm and cervical cap, there wasn't a lot left short of abstinence. I felt let down and angry at all the doctors who had nothing left to offer me. I didn't become pregnant through lack of knowledge, but lack of enthusiasm and energy to persevere with methods I couldn't accept.   *Liz*

Infertility

Sometimes we decide not to use contraception at all, or rely on a method which we know is not very safe because we believe we are not fertile. This belief may be based on the fact that we think we are too old or too young to conceive, or we may have had unprotected intercourse before and not conceived so we assume that we cannot be very fertile:

> I had stopped using the diaphragm for a few months because I wanted to be pregnant. Then I changed my

mind and started using it again. But I seemed to become less rigorous about it – possibly I'd come to believe I wasn't fertile anyway.   *Cath*

This feeling can be backed up by family history:

I had a fairly severe hormonal imbalance at the time and apart from being fed up with contraception, I didn't think I was fertile. (My sisters had had to have fertility injections in order to conceive.) I had asked for a fertility test, but you can only get them if you want children, not if you don't want to use contraception.   *Liz*

Being unprepared
Sometimes we choose not to obtain any contraception because we are afraid of having sex and believe that by not having contraception we cannot be forced into a sexual relationship we are not sure we want. As far as unexpected sexual encounters are concerned, women, rather than men, are expected to be responsible for 'protecting themselves'. Not surprisingly many of us reject this pressure.

The first time I conceived I had just finished a relationship with a woman, therefore I had no need of contraception. I had a one-night stand and, wham bam, I was pregnant.   *Sandra*

Wanting to be pregnant
At other times we do not use contraception because we want, either consciously or unconsciously, to become pregnant and it is only when we find out we have conceived that we decide we can't have a child at that time.

It was the result of intercourse with a long-term 'boyfriend, partner, lover', an act of folly, a one-off – 'it won't happen to me'. But I was wondering if it would, kind of hoping that it would. I had been using a cap successfully previous to my playing-with-fate episode.   *Janet*

I found myself much more sexually aroused when I wasn't using any method of contraception than when I was, so it was, more or less, in a strange sort of way, deliberate. Our children had grown up and I thought it would be very nice to have another baby. Thirty-nine is very much the last time, isn't it?   *Betty*

I'd come off the pill and he said, 'We'll give it a month and if you conceive in that time then fair enough, and if nothing happens you go back on it.' I didn't conceive in a month but I didn't go back on it and I didn't tell him and he didn't ask. It was like an unspoken thing between us and I knew deep down exactly what I was doing.   *Sandra*

Or we may become pregnant because we are badly in need of love and hope that having a baby would make our boyfriends or husbands love us more. If we are young and our parents do not have much time for us we may become pregnant either to gain their attention or to demonstrate that we are now grown up and no longer need their support. Sometimes we become pregnant in order to punish them.

As well as wanting to be loved, some of us also become pregnant because we want to give love to something that is ours and which no one can take away:

I suppose if I had a baby it would be something I could love and it would love me back and it would be mine and wonderful until it was sixteen when it would go, 'Ooh what an oppressive mother!'   *Sandra*

If we have become pregnant because we have felt deprived of either love or attention, but then decide we cannot go through with the pregnancy, we can often benefit from warm and supportive counselling before and after the abortion.

Contraceptive failure

Although we are encouraged to believe that if we use contraception conscientiously it is unlikely to let us down, the number of inexplicable failures is surprisingly high. Seven out of ten unwanted pregnancies are due to contraceptive failure, with condom failure the leading cause. No method of contraception, not even the pill, is 100 per cent effective. Consequently if we do become pregnant when we are using birth control we often experience great anger against the method which has failed us, the doctor who prescribed it, and sometimes against our body because we feel it has betrayed us.

The Pill

The contraceptive pill is the most popular form of contraception in Britain; it is used by 23 per cent of all women aged between 20 and 49. There are many kinds of contraceptive pill. These can be divided into the combined pill (combining the two hormones oestrogen and progestogen) and the mini-pill (progestogen only). Oestrogen prevents an egg from developing, while progestogen keeps the cervical mucus thick in order to form a 'plug' in the cervix to stop sperm entering the uterus.

The amount of both hormones in contraceptive pills has been greatly reduced since the first pills were produced. The progestogen used has also changed. During the 1980s second- and third-generation progestogens were introduced to try to lessen unwanted side effects. The third-generation pills were the subject of a scare concerning the increased risk of blood clots, as mentioned earlier in this chapter.

Although the pill is the most effective of all the methods – the combined pill being quoted as 99 to 99.9 per cent effective depending on the level of hormones in a particular brand, and 96 to 98 per cent safe for the mini-pill[15] – failures do occur. Sickness or diarrhoea can prevent hormones from being absorbed, and certain drugs are thought to reduce their effectiveness (particularly aspirin, anti-biotics and some tranquillisers). Occasionally, some women become pregnant while taking the pill because the hormone level of the particular brand they are taking is not high enough to prevent ovulation occurring.

Condoms

The condom (French letter, sheath, rubber) has a 98 per cent success rate when it is used with spermidical creams, jellies or pessaries which give extra protection if the rubber splits.[16]

Condoms are used by 15 per cent of women, including 1 per cent who use them with other methods of contraception. Condoms are particularly favoured by teenagers because they are widely available without prescription, and can be bought from vending machines. Nearly half of the young people visiting Brook Advisory Centres in 1995–96 chose condoms as their main method of contraception, compared with only 15 per cent in 1986. Condoms are particularly popular with the under 16s but in the last decade have been used more widely by all age groups, sometimes in conjunction with other methods of contraception, because of the protection they provide from sexually transmitted diseases such as HIV.

[There was] no obvious contraceptive failure. We had used the condom for four years conscientiously. *Sheila*

The female condom, marketed under the brand-name, Femidom, was introduced into Britain in 1992. It is used by fewer than 1 per cent of women, perhaps because it feels bulky and unwieldy to use, and it can be distractingly audible during sex! Its effectiveness ranges from 85 to 98 per cent depending on the use of adequate spermicide. Femidoms are available from pharmacies, but are more expensive than male condoms.

Diapraghms and cervical caps

Like the condom, diaphragms and cervical caps are said to be 98 per cent effective when used with a spermicide.[17] They need to be inserted before intercourse and should remain in place for at least six hours afterwards.

Although many people refer to all cervical-barrier methods as 'caps' there are in fact several different types. There is the diaphragm, which is a large rubber dome that fits over the cervix and is held in place by the pubic bone, and the smaller caps which fit over the cervix only, such as the vimule, the vault and the cervical cap. These should all be checked for size every six months as the vagina can change in shape. They should also be checked after 7 lb weight changes, after the birth of a baby, or a miscarriage or abortion.

> [I could never think of any] reason [for conception] as I was using the diaphragm correctly – I was. It was 'one of those things'. I might have a high fertility rate. *Ann*

> I made love in the bath! The consultant who I saw at the hospital said that I wasn't the first pregnancy that he'd seen as a result of doing this.   *Alice*

Intra-uterine device (IUD) or coil

There are several types of IUD which are commonly used. Although they are quoted as being between 96 and 98 per cent effective, no one knows exactly how they work and it is believed that their failure may be due to the fact that aspirin and antibiotics can lower their effectiveness. They can also be completely or partially rejected by the womb, especially in the first three months after insertion, so they need to be checked during the initial period before each time you have intercourse. After three months they should be checked after each menstrual period. If the womb is rejecting the coil you can normally feel a hard plastic end at the entrance to your cervix. Coils need to be changed every few years, depending on the type inserted, as the effectiveness decreases after that time.

If a pregnancy does occur when the IUD is in place you should always insist that the doctor who carries out the termination checks the uterine contents for foetal material, as IUDs can cause pregnancies in the Fallopian tube (ectopic pregnancy).

> When I discovered I was pregnant I felt absolutely furious that my IUD had failed . . . [I had feelings of] disbelief, fury at my GP for not checking my IUD properly when I had seen him over the past two months for problematic mid-cycle spotting caused by the IUD in the cervical canal!   *Patricia*

In 1995 a new IUD called Mirena became available. Mirena carries a store of the hormone progestogen, which is slowly released over three years. Because it acts locally, smaller doses are needed than with the pill. Menstrual loss is reduced with Mirena, but as with other IUDs, the main unwanted effect is irregular bleeding.

The Sponge

A contraceptive sponge was briefly available in the UK in the mid-1990s, but was taken off the market because of it's high failure rate.

Norplant

In 1993 a new method of contraception, Norplant, was launched in the UK. Norplant consists of six flexible capsules containing the hormonal contraceptive levonorgestrel, which are placed under the skin of the upper arm. The capsules remain in place for five years, during which time the woman can expect a high degree of protection from pregnancy (about 99 per cent) but may also experience menstrual disturbances – often heavier or more erratic bleeding – and other side effects such as acne and weight gain. More than 45,000 women chose this method between 1993 and 1996. A number of women have had their implants removed prematurely due to side effects, and some of these women have had further problems with difficult removals.

Injectable contraceptives

Although Depo-Provera has been in existence for several years it has only been approved for general use in the UK since 1995. It can now be offered to anyone asking about contraception. This method involves an injection of progestogen, usually into the buttocks, every 12 weeks. It is extremely effective – 99–100 per cent. The disadvantage is that if unacceptable side effects occur, such as excessive bleeding and weight gain, there is no means of removing the contraceptive before it is due to wear off.

Natural family planning (NFP)

Natural family planning (NFP), whereby we try to predict when we ovulate by taking our temperature or using the Billings method (noting the changes in our vaginal mucus and either abstaining from intercourse during the ten-day fertile period, or using contraception), has a high rate of failure, being listed as only 80 per cent effective in the first year.[18] Yet because it involves no mechanical devices or chemicals, and demands the participation of the male partner, it is the only method which is acceptable to some women. It is also the only method which is sanctioned by the Catholic Church and so is the choice of many women with strongly held Catholic beliefs.

One of the causes of the failure rate is the difficulty in knowing precisely when the 'safe period' occurs. Women who have irregular cycles or who do not check their temperature or mucus daily cannot tell when ovulation is taking place. Risk of conception is further increased by the fact that although the egg only survives for up to 24 hours, the sperm can survive for seven days or more.

> I thought my period had just finished and that it would be safe. In fact I later realised that it was more than five days finished. It was my first sexual encounter with full intercourse with a male.   *Nell*

> I became pregnant on honeymoon. I had calculated that I was within the safe period. However, I realised later I had not allowed for the life-span of sperm. *Vanessa*

> I was foolish enough, I suppose, to believe that I was capable of using the diaphragm only when I believed myself to be fertile – though I relied on cycle rather than cervical mucus or temperature. I believed it was a safe time for me.   *Val*

A new method to monitor fertility became available in Britain in 1996. The device, called Persona, is sold only through Boots chemists and consists of test sticks for sampling urine and a hand-held monitor which reads the test stick. The monitor shows a red light on fertile days and a green light on days when you are not fertile. The manufacturers claim that the system has an efficiency rate of 95 per cent.

Morning-after methods

Women who have had unprotected intercourse can try to prevent a possible pregnancy by two different methods. The first is the 'morning-after' pill. This involves obtaining four tablets of either Schering PC4 or *Ovran*

50 from a doctor or family planning clinic. These have to be taken within 72 hours of intercourse. Two tablets are taken as soon as possible, and another two are taken twelve hours later. Some doctors may refuse to prescribe these pills, in which case a woman can either insist on being referred to another doctor or can go to a Brook Clinic, abortion charity or family planning clinic that will prescribe it.

The method is 98 per cent effective. The main side effect is nausea, although this can be avoided by taking the tablets with food or with anti-nausea tablets, which may be prescribed at the same time. If bleeding does not occur or if your period is lighter than usual you should have a pregnancy test. If there is a pregnancy, there is no evidence that having taken the morning-after pill damages the foetus. You will be faced with exactly the same choices as any other woman with an unplanned pregnancy.

> [The] sheath split so I took the morning-after pill which didn't work. I had severe nausea and vomiting after four hours.   *Ros*

Women who have a history of high blood pressure, thrombosis or who have been advised not to take oral contraceptives should not take the morning-after pill, but should consider post-coital IUD insertion, which can also prevent a pregnancy in some cases. An IUD can be inserted up to ten days after intercourse but most doctors are hesitant to insert one after more than five days as it could be classed as an abortion if conception has taken place.

Being pregnant

Some of us know instinctively when we are pregnant, occasionally from the point of conception. Others, however, particularly those who do not menstruate regularly, may be unaware they have conceived for many weeks.

> I can remember distinctly feeling, 'That's it. I'm probably pregnant now.' I don't quite know whether or not it was a biological or mental reaction, but I remember it and that reaction/feeling very strongly. *Val*

> We had gone further than before, though had not had complete or full intercourse (not even proper penetration), but I remember lying in bed afterwards and knowing, really knowing without any shadow of a doubt that I had conceived.   *Rachel*

Changes in our body

Often the first indication that tells us that we are pregnant is that our body begins to react differently. Common symptoms of early pregnancy are amenorrhoea (missing a period), painful and swollen breasts, mild or severe nausea, more frequent urination, feeling tired, and altered bowel movements, We can experience all, some or none of these changes and, depending on our knowledge of pregnancy and our bodies, we often attach more significance to one symptom than to another.

Most of us, at some point in our lives, have experienced the fear that accompanies missing a period and, for those of us who have regular cycles, a missed period can be the first sign that we have conceived. At about the same time we may experience swollen, tingling, painful or throbbing breasts caused by the developing milk glands. Our nipples and the area around them may darken and become broader, while the increased blood supply to our breasts can make the veins more prominent:

> My period was late but I didn't go on that alone as I

had never kept a check on it. I had great difficulty afterwards convincing myself that there was some correlation between sexual experiences, periods and pregnancy. It was a splintered connection. The definite jolt to go and find out if I was or wasn't was when my breasts enlarged as I had always had a rather small bust and was rather conscious of it.   *Marie*

I missed a period and felt very pre-menstrual and had breast discomfort. This became more noticeable about two weeks from the date of my first missed period.   *Joyce*

Another common symptom is nausea or 'morning sickness'. The degree to which women experience nausea varies. Those who suffer from it often find it can be alleviated by eating dry toast or crackers slowly in the morning, taking vitamin B6 and avoiding spiced or greasy food.

The trouble with pregnancy is that you get sick and you feel so rotten, or maybe you don't if it's planned – you push it to one side. I mean with my two kiddies I had in the early days I don't feel I felt the impact of the illness. Maybe being older made it worse. I remember I felt absolutely nauseous.   *Betty*

I had morning sickness from the fourth week of pregnancy. Because I had never felt like that before I had a strong suspicion I must be pregnant. I had breast changes at about the same time.   *Sheila*

Although some of us don't experience morning sickness we may notice that our body yearns for different foods or develops an aversion to particular types of food. Another sign of pregnancy is wanting to urinate more frequently. Slight abdominal pains, similar to those experienced before a period, may also be felt. These are caused by the stretching of the uterus and are likely to be more noticeable if a pelvic infection in the past has caused scarring.

Not knowing we are pregnant

Some of us experience these symptoms but do not always relate them to pregnancy. We can therefore be unaware we have conceived for some time. Women who have been using contraception, for instance, can find it very hard to believe their method has failed them. One woman who was using the cap wrote:

> I'd missed a period but thought this was due to emotional upheaval and the fact that I had moved away to live in Cornwall for the summer. It was suggested to me by a woman I was working with that I should buy a testing kit. I thought she was daft but did it anyway.   *Alice*

Some of us ignore the symptoms because we don't feel we can cope with the pregnancy, or face up to a termination, and by pushing it to the back of our minds we hope the problem will go away.

> My periods didn't come on and I suppose I did have all the symptoms, my breasts started to hurt and I started eating bread and jam at very odd hours of the morning, but I think my mind was just saying, 'I can't cope with this.' I mean because the one [before] had just been in December.   *Sandra*

Women who have irregular periods – because they have only recently begun to menstruate or are approaching the menopause or who have irregular or long cycles – may not receive any indication that they are pregnant for some time because they do not expect to menstruate on a particular day. Furthermore some of the symptoms of pregnancy, such as swollen breasts, irritability, abdominal pain and tiredness, are very similar to pre-menstrual syndrome (PMS), and we may often think that we are about to start bleeding.

Looking back, I had a lot of the signs: no period, swollen breasts, abdominal pains, water retention. I even remember saying to a male friend who noticed that my breasts were large, that it was usual for me, it was all part of PMS. I made a joke about 'nature's own silicone injections'.   *Liz*

It is possible that bleeding may occur and be confused with a period. Although this bleeding is usually short, if it is unaccompanied by any other symptoms we can be unaware of having conceived for several months.

The main reason I didn't know I was pregnant was because I was still having normal periods and didn't notice any difference in myself until I was on holiday and missed two periods. When I came back I had put on nearly two stone and my breasts were bigger. I was 24 weeks pregnant.   *Sally*

Waiting

I was very concerned and depressed. Although subconsciously I knew I was pregnant I tried to think (to force myself to think) that I probably wasn't and that my period would start tomorrow.   *Vanessa*

The waiting time between believing we are pregnant because that is what our mind and our body are telling us and having the pregnancy medically confirmed can be a difficult period. We oscillate between thinking we are not and fearing that we may be. The state of knowing, yet not knowing, can make us feel powerless, angry and distressed. It can also be the time when we begin to come to terms with what a pregnancy would mean to us.

When it suddenly occurred to me that I was probably pregnant, I felt both excited and terrified. Sort of,

'Well if I'm pregnant, it's rather wonderful, I can have babies, I'm a proper woman!' But also, 'If I'm pregnant I'll have to get an abortion and I wonder how I'll cope?' I was very strung up and kept praying to God for it all to be a bad dream.   *Liz*

Pregnancy tests

As soon as we suspect that we are pregnant it is advisable to seek medical confirmation. The earlier a pregnancy is confirmed, the more time we have to decide whether we want to continue with it or to terminate it. If we decide on a termination, the earlier the operation is performed, the safer and less physically traumatic it is. Making an early decision also gives a woman more time to make arrangements for travelling to another country if the abortion laws are restrictive in her own.

When you are pregnant certain hormones are present in your urine and blood. There are various ways of testing for these hormones, and pregnancy tests can now be done from the first day of a missed period, although the British Pregnancy Advisory Service suggests that you wait until your period is about four days late before deciding to have a test.

Where to get a pregnancy test

Pregnancy tests are carried out in doctors' surgeries, family planning clinics, well-woman centres, and pregnancy advisory centres. Many pharmacies offer a pregnancy testing service, and also sell home pregnancy testing kits.

Home pregnancy testing kits

Home pregnancy testing kits cost about £8 to £12 and are about 99 per cent accurate if the instructions are followed carefully. They involve testing your early-morning urine by watching for colour changes either in a test stick or in a test slide. The disadvantage of home testing is that you are on your own with the result, unless you have told a friend or family member that you are doing the test. Most pregnancy testing services available from doctors or clinics, and from some pharmacies, offer information on counselling and practical help. But some women prefer to be the first to know about their pregnancy. After doing a home pregnancy test many women seek confirmation of the result by going to a clinic or their GP.

GPs

Some GPs and health centres will carry out pregnancy tests on the spot. However, if you have only just missed a period, or if they do not provide this facility, your urine sample will be sent to a hospital laboratory. Insist on being given the result as soon as your GP receives it. *There is no need for you to have to wait weeks.*

Some women, however, don't want to involve their GP in their pregnancy and prefer to use other sources.

Pharmacies

Pharmacies which provide a pregnancy testing service usually advertise the service in their shop window. They are normally quick and you can get the results in around two to three hours. The fee for testing is about £10. If your local pharmacy does not offer this service, ask for the nearest one which does.

Family planning clinics, Brook Advisory Centres, abortion charities

Some family planning clinics, Brook Advisory Centres, the Pregnancy Advisory Service (PAS) and the British Pregnancy Advisory Service (BPAS) will do pregnancy testing on the spot. For a list of addresses, telephone numbers and costs see Appendix 2.

DSS-approved pregnancy advisory bureaux

Private organisations which have been approved by the DSS to act as pregnancy advisory bureaux offer pregnancy testing services, as well as pregnancy counselling and abortion provision (see Appendix 2 for addresses).

Commercial agencies

Commercial pregnancy testing services are run by some laboratories which advertise in women's magazines and the Yellow Pages.

Postal tests

BPAS branches, Marie Stopes, the well women centres and Open Line Counselling, Dublin, all offer postal pregnancy tests and will give the results by phone. If at all possible it is better to obtain a test which does not involve postage, as delays can mean that the sample deteriorates and gives a false reading. For women who live in rural areas, however, this may be the only practical course of action.

LIFE

LIFE offers pregnancy testing services and counselling, but the organisation concentrates on helping women continue with their pregnancies. If you want an abortion it is better to ge a clinic that specialises in abortion services.

Urine tests

Urine tests are used by most hospitals, pregnancy advisory bureaux, chemists, some commercial laboratories and those GPs and family planning clinics that have the facilities to carry out a test. All pregnancy tests of urine done by GPs, clinics and pharmacies use the same method as the home testing kit. You will need to take a sample of your early-morning urine in a clean jar. The result may be more accurate than a home test because the person doing the test is used to the procedure. Most of the tests performed are slide tests, although some hospitals use more complex tests involving radioactive chemicals. The advantage of the slide test is that a reading can be obtained within minutes and the results given straight away. The disadvantage is that the type of test which many centres use will only register a reliable result 14 days after the first day of the missed period.

False readings

My periods stopped and I had a test done two weeks after and they said it was negative and I said, 'Shall I come back?', and they said, 'No'.   *Sandra*

Although most pregnancy tests are very reliable, false positive and false negative readings can and do occur. Inaccurate readings occur for a number of reasons, including errors during the storage of testing agents, a urine sample that is too old or has been kept too long at room temperature, contamination of the urine container or testing equipment, or because you have not been pregnant for as long as you believed and do not have a high enough concentration of pregnancy hormones in the sample. This last reason is often the case with women who have long or irregular cycles, or who cannot remember the date of the first day of their last period and ask for a test too soon. A false negative reading can also occur if you have an ectopic (outside the womb) pregnancy, or if you are more than 16 weeks pregnant when the level of pregnancy hormones tends to drop. Symptoms of ectopic pregnancy are abdominal pain which may be worse on one side and may be sudden and severe, bleeding, and signs of shock such as pallor and faintness. If this happens, see a doctor immediately.

False negatives are much less likely to happen with the more sensitive, earlier slide tests. This test is also unlikely to give false positive readings for menopausal women and those taking oral contraceptives or other drugs where additional substances in the urine can confuse the reacting agents.

If you do not receive a negative result don't let anyone talk you into believing you aren't pregnant if you really feel you are, but insist on having another test a week later. If that proves negative, insist on a third test. If you are still getting a negative result but firmly believe you are pregnant ask your doctor for a further test. She or he may try to imply that you are being fanciful, but it's your body, and you know it better than anyone else.

> I went to my GP twelve days after I was overdue. He was very unhelpful and told me it was just nerves and to come back next month if I didn't come on. I told him I *knew* I was pregnant and didn't want to wait. He told me that I shouldn't tell a pilot how to fly a plane.
> *Margo*

Stage of pregnancy

Although a pregnancy test can tell us whether we are pregnant or not, it cannot determine how many weeks pregnant we actually are. If we have only had sexual intercourse on one occasion we should be able to pinpoint the date exactly. Otherwise, pregnancy is calculated from the number of weeks that have elapsed since the first day of our last menstrual period (LMP). If a pregnancy test gives a positive result two weeks after the first day of our missed period, therefore, we are said to be six weeks pregnant. All references to the stage of pregnancy in this book are based on LMP.

Most doctors follow this standard although there are a few who use their own methods of calculation. If the estimated stage of pregnancy is not based on LMP we should question the figure given since the number of weeks can decide the type of abortion we have (p94 *Medical Techniques of Abortion*).

Pregnancies are also divided into 'trimesters', the first being up to 14 weeks LMP, the second between 15 and 28 weeks LMP, and the third 29 weeks and over.

Getting the result

Our initial reactions on learning that we are pregnant can vary enormously. Some of us are so sure we are pregnant that the result is no surprise, while others feel incredibly relieved or shocked, angry, frightened or confused. Often we are surprised by the way we react as it is not how we imagined we would feel. If we think we are going to be upset it can help to have a strong woman friend with us when we are given the result.

For some women a positive result brings feelings of relief. It marks the end of a period of powerlessness when they have not known what is happening to them and therefore have been unable to take action. Knowing that they are pregnant allows them to start taking control over their lives and bodies again.

The reactions of other women can be very different. Being pregnant without choosing to be can make us feel we have no control over our bodies, and therefore brings back feelings that we may have suffered before, either as children or as women trying to gain recognition for ourselves in environments where women are not valued. If we are used to feeling we have no control, or have constantly had to battle for our needs and rights, this feeling can manifest itself as a feeling of inevitability.

I don't think I felt guilty about letting myself get into

that position. It's very odd, it's almost as if I'd known all my life that this would happen to me. I can't think of any other way of describing it: it's like my life, it's been a lot of battles right the way through and in a way it was like, 'Well of course I'm going to be put through this as well.' And I don't mean to sound like a big martyr, like I've had such a hard life and so I'm bound to have this other, but that's what I felt about it. Of course, this bloody thing's going to be lumped on me as well, on top of everything else. Now someone's decided I'm fertile. Wham!   *Sandra*

Sometimes this feeling of not being in control is symbolised by feeling we have been invaded by an uninvited guest:

I felt appalled. I felt I had been taken over by an 'alien something' that was then using me to feed off and grow.   *Ann*

Some women feel that the pregnancy is a punishment, often as a result of early guilty feelings about our sexuality:

I felt I had been 'punished' or 'caught out' and, probably for the first time in my adult life, I felt I was not in control of what was happening to me.   *Margo*

Our lack of control can cause us to feel very, very angry and make us want to hit out to prove that we are still capable of action.

When I was handed the form with a tick in the positive box I felt terribly angry. I screwed it up in a ball and threw it on the floor and said, 'Shit!' and wanted everyone to hear me. When I got outside the chemist I realised I would probably need it and went back. I felt very weird. Out of control, high and my hands were shaking. Then I wanted to laugh hysterically.   *Liz*

Many of us will understandably feel betrayed by our

bodies and our contraception:

> [I felt] immense anger and betrayal. Also somewhat stunned. My anger had something to do with feeling let down by my method of contraception as I had been so careful for so many years.   *Isobel*

Because as women we are so used to being expected to take the blame for everything, we often turn this anger in on ourselves, or allow ourselves to feel that it is 'our fault' rather than blaming our contraception or expecting our partner to take equal responsibility.

> I was angry at myself for allowing it to happen. I was angry at my boyfriend. I was angry at just about everyone but I didn't fully understand all the ins and outs of all that was happening.   *Sally*

Some of us find the reality of being pregnant too much to take in immediately, and receive the results with disbelief ('I thought they were joking': *Janet*). We often hope that it is not true, that the pregnancy will somehow go away and we shall never have to face up to deciding whether to have an abortion or not.

If we are living with our parents, or in a society which condemns abortion and pregnancy outside of marriage, one of our first reactions may be fear that we shall be 'found out'. We may worry that we may have to admit we have been having sexual relations to people we know will not be sympathetic.

Living with our pregnancy

The ways in which we experience and cope with being pregnant are very different: we may view the situation calmly and make plans for a termination; we may not think about it a great deal; or we may try and distance ourselves from it in order to be able to cope with day-today life and responsibilities. Alternatively we may experience a whole range of conflicting emotions that confuse us and are difficult to understand.

One of the hardest feelings to come to terms with is being happy about being pregnant while at the same time knowing that we do not want, or cannot have, a child at that time. The feelings of joy and elation are entirely natural for many of us. Since childhood we have been conditioned into viewing motherhood as an achievement, a sign of maturity, fullness and independence from the family that nurtured us. We may disagree with these traditional assumptions of our role but, if we have retained vestiges of our conditioning, these may surface at this point. If we have had children before and enjoyed the experience of pregnancy and childbirth, or if we have felt strong urges to have a child in the past, then the feeling of happiness can be very strong:

> [My feelings were] quite a mixture – I felt excitement at being pregnant for the first time and happy. But also anxious because the father and I had decided not to have a baby by then and he wanted me to have an abortion. I was distressed when I realised what I had to do.   *Cath*

> [I was] happy in a way – but I had a feeling of dread and disbelief in the back of my mind. I do have a strong desire for a child, but I was also very aware of the practical and emotional implications. Also my work is involved with babies so I was unable to forget it for a moment.   *Sheila*

Some of us start to develop a relationship with the developing life inside us:

> I certainly felt some emotional disturbance. I felt close to the child I was carrying. I remember looking in books at how developed the baby was; what organs

would have formed at ten weeks.   *Theresa*

The pregnancy can make us feel joyful because it is proof that we are fertile. Being pregnant can also make us much more aware of our body and more sensitive to our environment. Some of us enjoy this greater perception, but others feel more vulnerable and emotional. One unasked-for event has happened and thus we are wary of more 'accidents' occurring.

I couldn't think of anything else. The thought of my pregnancy overlaid everything. I hated being in the dark – something not experienced before or since – it made me feel claustrophobic.   *Margo*

For some of us the situation is just too painful so we automatically shut off from it. Feelings of unreality, being in a dream, and being numb are very common and can stay with us right up to, and after, the abortion:

I was probably severely depressed because I felt nothing at all. I was unable to cry, felt like a zombie, drained of any ability to feel or think.   *Chris*

[I felt] quite numb, but not totally. I even remember feeling joyful and proud at one time and also quite desperate, but it wasn't until afterwards that I could see clearly what was happening. There is a bit of fear of the unknown.   *Theresa*

Other women cope with this period by adopting a protective role. Although this can help us through a difficult time, it can also be damaging as it can make us sacrifice how we really feel and prevent us from asking for the help we need.

On the other hand I felt like an actress, like everyone was watching me and waiting to see how I would react. So I put on one hell of a performance. On the other hand I was deeply hurt, because the father had left me to cope alone and I was scared and frightened. But I distanced myself from my feelings and from everyone else by playing the superwoman role: 'Look at me, I'm pregnant and I'm still working nine hours a day and then go out and socialise and make you laugh and listen to your problems instead of boring on about mine. Aren't I doing well?'   *Liz*

Women who live in a country where abortion is illegal, or are resident in one where they do not know the laws, can find that worries about how they are going to obtain an abortion overshadow or mingle with their other feelings:

I was in England only six months and I did not know the system [in Canada legal abortion was very difficult at that time] and I was frightened I might not be able to get a legal abortion and might have to resort to a back-street one.   *Janice*

Some of us just want to get it over with, so that all the pain will be taken away:

[I was] terribly anxious and upset – butterflies and churning stomach – just wanted to be out of the situation – probably rather a childish reaction – it hurt and I just wanted it to be over, for someone else to take the pain away.   *Rachel*

Telling others

An important part of coming to terms with our pregnancy is being able to talk to other people about what is happening to us. By sharing our feelings with them and accepting their love and caring we no longer feel we are alone with our problem and often feel more able to cope. We normally choose to confide in people we know we can trust and who will not try to make us feel guilty about our pregnancy and our feelings that we may not wish to continue with it. Generally we need both sympathy and emotional and practical support. If we do not get both we can feel let down and hurt:

> I actually chose to confide in a friend from school who, being a contemporary, was not going to be shocked. She tried to be helpful and sympathetic but could do nothing and I didn't feel any support from her.   *Rachel*

If we are in an established relationship one of the first people we turn to is the person with whom we became pregnant or, if we are lesbians, to our lover. Some men can be very warm and caring and this can give us a great deal of strength when we are deciding what we want to do. For some men, however. responding to our needs at this time seems almost impossible. Fear of commitment, of responsibility, of our feelings and of being faced with a decision involving potential life, can result in panic, disbelief and sometimes rejection. At this time, friends who can 'be there' for us are invaluable:

> [I confided] initially as I needed to borrow money and to have somewhere to stay in London. I subsequently discussed the experience at length with a close woman friend and this helped to make it a learning process. Both friends were very supportive and non-judgemental. My friend in London is a gentle gay male and my woman friend has since given birth joyously. *Isobel*

> [I told my] woman friends who were sympathetic, supportive and understanding. I did not tell the man as the relationship had finished. I did tell him later, just before the abortion, as I thought he ought to know but I didn't ask anything of him – there wasn't anything I needed from him.   *Ann*

As well as wanting support and comfort, we sometimes want to speak to someone who is outside our immediate circle and can be objective about our situation, thereby putting it in perspective and often giving us practical information we may not have:

I talked to a friend and she was the first person who was very honest with me. She said, 'Look, what are you doing, do you want this kid or what?' And she was just very straight and very direct and it was so helpful because everyone around me had been involved right from the start and were caught up in the same emotional feelings of indecision as I was. *Sandra*

If we want, or need, to keep our pregnancy a secret then whom we tell is normally determined by knowing who will respect our confidence.

I told two close friends. One who loaned me £40 and one whose sister loaned me the rest. These friends were unutterably discreet, loyal, sympathetic and supportive, and also kept it totally secret as I was a very public figure in college [it was before the 1967 Abortion Act]. *Nell*

Because the support of our women friends is so important, one of the worst experiences about an abortion can be if they let us down when we really need them. Often they may have their own reasons for not being able to help us, but because our worries are so pressing we may not be able to recognise how they feel.

[I told] a friend I was sharing the house with. I wanted to tell someone and, prior to our stay in Cyprus, we had been very trustful and sincere with each other. But she was living with one of the two other guys in the house and he wasn't treating her very well so her relationship with me deteriorated as I wasn't very supportive to her with her problems. I wasn't in fact aware that things were bad between them, so it was a chance of telling someone who might sympathise. She didn't. She was very distant. Her lover and the other guy were very sympathetic. *Marie*

Sometimes we tell people because we feel so special about what is happening to us that we want them to share in our joy and excitement:

I phoned two friends in London who were calm and supportive. One of them congratulated me on my achievement once she'd realised I wasn't distressed but excited! *Val*

Should an unplanned pregnancy occur at a time when life is going wrong for us in several important ways, we may tell people about it as a way of getting the recognition we lack in other areas. Although at some point we have to face up to our lack of fulfilment, any love and caring given to us at this time can give us the confidence we need.

I confided in just about everyone, except my parents and sisters. I did want support and my friends and workmates gave it to me in abundance. But I also wanted attention. I now realise I partly used the pregnancy and later the abortion to get recognition I wasn't getting in my work and in my relationship. *Liz*

Young women living with parents who they believe would be shocked by their pregnancy can find it very difficult to tell anyone because they are terrified of being 'found out' or, worse, of being 'thrown out'. When this happens it is often helpful to be able to tell someone who is older who can help us tell our parents.

I confided in my youth centre warden, who was a woman and who knew the best place to go. She was very supportive and came to see my foster parents with me and helped me explain what I was going to do.

Because [my foster parents] were Catholic I found it very hard.   *Sally*

Once our parents know we are pregnant we can feel ill-at-ease and unable to talk to them about how we really feel:

My mother found out and was supportive, coming with me to doctors etc., but unsympathetic at first and rather distant and shocked. I wanted to talk to someone who was as concerned about me as my mum, but more sympathetic, and to whom I could talk without the trappings of guilt that come with a shocked member of the family.   *Rachel*

There are often people whom we are close to, and whom we trust, but whom we can't confide in because we believe they would be too distressed.

I had this almost insatiable urge to tell my very Catholic family which is, I suppose, bound up in how intrinsically I feel they don't know me. It wasn't a sadistic urge, rather that something extremely important was happening to me, something very thrilling and I couldn't share it.   *Val*

Not telling our family, or more particularly our mothers, can be very painful. Our mother represents, either symbolically or literally, the all-caring figure who can ease away all our hurt and pain. To realise, often for the first time, that you can no longer depend on her for support is to accept you are no longer a child but an independent woman with responsibility for your own life. The experience is essentially a very positive one, but at the same time can be very isolating.

I would have liked to have been able to confide in my mother. I wanted to be able to say, 'Look, I'm grown up, let's talk about how we both feel about pregnancy.'

But I also wanted to be able to crawl into her lap like I did when I was sick and a little girl and cry and cry and cry. One night I felt so bad I nearly did ring her. Now I'm glad I didn't.   *Liz*

Other women find it easier to come to terms with their pregnancy by telling no one, or telling only a few people:

I didn't really want to talk to anyone about it. I wished the whole thing over with and my grief and anguish were intensely, privately, my own.   *Chris*

If a woman does not have any of the obvious symptoms of pregnancy it is quite easy to keep it hidden. For women who suffer badly from nausea, feel faint and generally look unwell, it can be impossible. Some women feel so vulnerable they avoid social contacts or take time off work. This can not only be difficult to account for, but can result in feeling ashamed that we have to keep it a secret.

I was sick and needed the loo. There was a complete change in my eating habits. It was a problem trying to pretend that everything was fine and normal, both at home and at work. I looked so *ill* that people knew something was wrong.   *Chris*

Once we have come to terms with our pregnancy and have felt able to talk about it with someone close to us, we are then in a position to take the next important step – deciding whether or not to continue with the pregnancy.

2
Deciding to Have an Abortion

It was the right decision but that doesn't mean I don't
sometimes regret and feel sad about it and think about
the baby and what might have been.   *Rachel*

Deciding to have an abortion is rarely an easy process,
and once the operation has taken place, our decision
cannot be reversed. Consequently it is important that we
allow ourselves time to explore our thoughts and feelings
very deeply before deciding what to do. We may also
want to consider alternatives to termination such as
adoption or having the baby brought up by a relative.

Our decision involves far more than deciding whether
it is possible for us to have a child, or another child, at a
particular point in our lives. We have to face fundamental issues of life, death, sexuality and motherhood.
Our intimate relationships will be challenged on many
fronts, and feelings of insecurity and uncertainty are
frequently experienced. Having to face such complex
issues when we are physically and emotionally

vulnerable demands a lot of strength, and we need to make sure we have the right amount of space for ourselves and support during this period.

Why we choose abortion

Choosing to have an abortion generally involves weighing up one set of factors against another in an attempt to find out which course of action is the more realistic. Different issues will obviously be more crucial to some women than to others. In listing the reasons that were important to the women who contributed to this book, no precedence is implied by the order in which they are examined.

Work

If we are pursuing, or are anxious to pursue, a job which brings us a great deal of satisfaction and fulfilment, then this will be a major factor in our decision-making. As soon as we realise that we are pregnant, we may know that we cannot combine motherhood with work, or we may need to spend time evaluating how important this part of our life is to us. Such consideration can often result in our taking a new look at our jobs and thus heightens our expectations of what we want.

> I wanted to be a PE teacher and didn't want anything to get in the way, especially without a father as I don't think it right to bring up children without both parents.   *Sally*

> It's always been unfortunate that every time I've been pregnant I've always been involved in a show, and that always takes priority . . . [When I had the second abortion] I went to see a show which I liked, it was very physical and I thought, 'I'd like to do something like that, maybe I'll do a street show.' And then I

thought, 'Oh no! You'll be eight months pregnant by then', and it went pow! in my head. It was that night I made the decision.   *Sandra*

The relationship with the father

When we are in a stable relationship with the father of the child, our feelings for this person and the way we see the partnership developing often influence the decision. If we are in a relationship that is special to us in some way, we may choose to have an abortion because we know it is not the right stage to include a third person.

I felt sure I wouldn't be able to cope by myself, either emotionally or practically. I was worried that if I continued with the pregnancy it would mess up any chance of having a good relationship with the father. He had been a good friend for one and a half years and I was worried that he would feel a sense of obligation to me.   *Alice*

I did not want a child and I was in a relationship which was new and was very important (we subsequently married), but I did not want to have to conduct it on the basis of being a family.   *Janice*

If the partnership is failing in some way, or if the father does not want to have a child, we may choose to have an abortion not only because we do not want to be a one-parent family, but also because we need to have time to sort out our feelings for the person and decide whether we want the relationship to continue.

The father made it clear that he wouldn't support me to have a child. I couldn't face single parenthood or losing the relationship. I felt bitter about the pressure from him, although I didn't realise this fully until later. *Cath*

I would have had the child with his support I think. Also I had the fear of having damaged the foetus through excessive alcohol at the very beginning before I knew I was pregnant (I was on holiday in Spain!). This was a bit of rationalisation though – I don't think it would have been a serious consideration if circumstances were different. [There was the] added difficulty of being a single, white parent to a black child – my boyfriend is black – he pushed this point *very* strongly.   *Sheila*

Not wanting children

Some of us decide to have an abortion because we don't want to have children. If we have not realised this about ourselves before we face an unplanned pregnancy we may, at first, find it difficult to come to terms with. Many people still find it hard to accept that some women simply do not want children, and they can react with hostility.

When we married we decided that we did not want children. As sterilisation is not given freely (metaphorically speaking) to women in their early twenties with no children, we decided to use adequate contraception. There is also the fact that neither of us wanted to interrupt our careers and perhaps that comes before not wanting children.   *Patricia*

Women who already have children are aware of the time and energy a baby demands and may neither want, nor be able, to give it:

When I first discovered I was pregnant I was horrified. I was a widow with two small boys aged six and eight in the spring of 1966 (quite enough to handle on my own) and in my second year of a teacher training course.   *Barbara*

My son was ten at the time [and] I'd just started a degree after years of badly paid shit work and was not prepared to interrupt it.   *Cheryl*

We had completed our family, our youngsters being then 12, 14 and 16. I had only recently completed a course and started a 'second life'.   *Jean*

Single parenthood

Other women decide on abortion because they don't want to be a single parent. Lone parents are undervalued and scape-goated in our society, which is geared to two-parent families. Many single mothers have found that the Child Support Agency is not as supportive as they hoped it would be. The CSA forces fathers to pay maintenance by bringing them to court. However, for women on benefits there is no gain because they lose pound for pound – every pound they gain in maintenance, they lose off their benefits. Bringing up a baby alone requires a great deal of strength which not all of us possess:

I suppose I didn't want an interruption of my life as I thought it might unfold – always having a 'good time' and out enjoying myself, but I do believe basically it was shameful to have a child outside of marriage and the prejudices that existed in Cyprus and Ireland did not create an atmosphere of acceptance for me. *Marie*

[I had] no visible means of support. [My] boyfriend was totally against the idea of me having the baby [and my] father would have been initially very shocked and outraged. I felt a bit weak-willed and pliable.   *Janet*

Fear of pregnancy and childbirth

Pregnancy and childbirth can be traumatic experiences. Women who have suffered badly with a previous pregnancy, or who have suffered severe post-natal depression, may decide to have an abortion rather than risk a similar experience:

> At 41, with an appalling obstetric history behind me, I found myself seven weeks pregnant. The thought of another attempt at child-bearing gave me no joy, as sixteen years ago I had a 43-week stillborn child born dead because, despite 'intensive' ante-natal care, I was induced to labour and to bear a child which would not physically fit through my pelvis! It was a nightmare which I did not relish the thought of repeating . . . I was not prepared to subject myself again to another experience of childbirth.   *Joyce*

> I have never wished to give birth. I have often considered that I might, in more personally settled times, foster a child.   *Isobel*

Too many responsibilities

As women we can find ourselves surrounded by so many responsibilities that we simply cannot cope with the added demands of caring for a child and therefore an abortion is the only course of action open to us:

> [At the time of my second abortion] I had an unstable relationship with my husband. I couldn't rely on him. My mother was living with me who had terminal cancer. I couldn't face the additional upheaval and trauma of another baby. I felt my mother might worry for me. And I can't afford not to be at work, I was frightened of my position – I knew I'd be vulnerable if I took leave.   *Janet*

> I was teaching drama, which was relatively lucrative and had just started to support my boyfriend for a year while he did further study (he had supported me previously). I felt it was my obligation to continue supporting him.   *Theresa*

Health issues

In some cases circumstances which are beyond our control can limit, or completely take away, our freedom of choice. In instances of very poor health, or as a result of an accident, an abortion may be necessary in order to save our lives. Similarly, if we are told the foetus is so damaged that it would not survive birth, then we have very little control over whether we have an abortion or not.

Where the foetus would survive birth, but the baby is likely to have impairment, we have a choice whether or not we could cope with a disabled child. Many disabled women have argued that abortion on the grounds of disability – and particularly the legal position whereby the disabled foetus can be aborted up to a much later stage in pregnancy – devalues disabled people's lives. (Books on this issue are included in the further reading list.) Making a decision on these grounds is always very painful as it has to be made after we have spent several months looking forward to the birth of a baby and we may experience considerable guilt about not feeling strong enough to care for a child that would be differently abled from ourselves.

About 10 per cent of abortions are carried out after 12 weeks of pregnancy, with almost all of these occurring between 13 and 19 weeks. The most common reason for these later abortions is that women initially accept the pregnancy, but then change their minds; this is sometimes due to a diagnosis of foetal impairment.[1] Recent advances in medical technology have improved the diagnosis of genetic and structural problems in the foetus. We now have greater choice over whether to continue with an affected pregnancy, often at an earlier stage of the pregnancy. Between 1971 and 1995 the proportion of abortions between 13 and 19 weeks more than halved, while the proportion of earlier abortions more than doubled.[2] Although the greater availability of tests does offer us more choice, we should always make sure that we understand what the tests involve and what they are for. Having a test does not mean consenting to an abortion if the results show that the foetus is affected. Some of the more common tests include:

Ultrasound scans

The greatest change in recent years has been in ultrasound scanning technology. Transvaginal scans – done with a probe in the vagina – allow the diagnosis of structural problems in the foetus at around 12–13 weeks' pregnancy. This is a big improvement on the previous choice of ultrasound at 18-20 weeks and a late abortion if impairment was found. Also at 10-13 weeks the new technique of nuchal translucency measurement with transvaginal and the older transabdominal scans can be used to identify the risk of Down's syndrome in the foetus.

Triple testing

At 15–16 weeks a routine blood test called the triple test can identify your risk of having a child affected by Down's syndrome and neural tube defects such as spina bifida. If the blood test indicates a certain level of risk, you will then be offered more invasive tests.

Invasive testing

Tests such as amniocentesis chorion villus sampling and cordocentesis are offered to women who are at greater risk of carrying a foetus with genetic disorders such as Down's syndrome, spina bifida and sickle cell disorders. These tests give a more definite result than scans and blood tests can, but also increase the risk of miscarriage and foetal impairment.

Most women find that counselling before and after each stage of testing and diagnosis helps them to think through their choices and to fully understand the nature of the results. The organisation Support After Termination of Pregnancy (SAFTA) offers information and support to women going through this process.

HIV

Routine testing for the Human Immunodeficiency Virus (HIV) is offered to pregnant women in the UK only in areas that have high prevalence for the virus, such as parts of London. The BPAS clinics do not screen women for HIV. Women who have HIV face the same questions as any other women when they discover they are pregnant. Having the virus (being HIV positive) is not a reason for automatically choosing abortion. By 1996 nearly 600 HIV positive women had given birth in Britain and Ireland.[3] Improved drugs and careful medical attention during birth can reduce the likelihood of transmission of the virus to the baby to about 8 per cent,[4] and there is no evidence that pregnancy affects the rate of positive progression to AIDS in women who have no symptoms. Nevertheless, nearly half of the HIV positive women in a 1994 survey stated that they had been pressured either not to become pregnant or to have an abortion if they were pregnant.[5] If you choose abortion you do not have to tell anyone about your status, as routine hygiene measures are adequate to prevent the spread of HIV during the abortion, although you may wish to disclose your status for other reasons. If you are HIV positive and pregnant you may find it helpful to talk to other women who have been in a similar situation. Groups such as Positively Women in London, or the Women and Aids Network in Scotland provide useful points of contact.

Rape

If we have become pregnant as a result of being raped we may choose abortion because we don't want to bear the child of a man who has brutalised us and which would be a constant reminder of our assault. Although we were victims during the attack, we are not powerless when it comes to deciding whether to continue with or terminate the pregnancy. Once we have come to terms with realising that an unwanted pregnancy need not be an extension of the powerlessness we experienced, the knowledge that the choice is ours can help to restore our sense of control. Rape Crisis Centres can offer emotional support.

Incest

Continuing with a pregnancy that arises from an incestuous relationship is not easy. Often the relationship has been one of coercion and has been conducted in secret, and we are scared that our mother, other family members or friends will find out. Making the decision to have an abortion, having to cope with all the arrangements, often when we find it too painful to explain to the doctors the real reasons for wanting a termination, can be extremely isolating if we have no one to turn to. There are various incest survivors helplines and other support services, a list of which can be found in the Resources section. These can help women with all aspects of coping with an unwanted pregnancy.

Making the decision

When deciding whether to have an abortion, we may or may not want to take into account the views of others. Some women, regardless of whether they are married or single, believe that only they can make the decision, while others feel that the father of the child, a lesbian lover, or their parents should participate in the decision-making.

Making the decision by ourselves

It was all my own decision. A decision based on my life at that time and on my preconceptions of what I would do if I became pregnant when I hadn't chosen to be. An abortion and not a baby seemed more realistic as I was single and not planning on marriage. I was angry that the father wasn't around so I could let him know what I was planning to do, but if he had been I would not have taken his views into account.   *Liz*

When the pregnancy has been the result of an unimportant sexual encounter, or has occurred at the end of a relationship, we may not feel any need to tell the father about either the pregnancy or the termination. If the relationship has not been a close one, involving the father can seem pointless, since we neither know nor trust him. Alternatively, if the relationship has finished it may be too painful for us to re-establish contact with someone we have agreed not to share our lives with anymore, and we may prefer to turn to our friends instead.

Some women feel that they need space in order to make up their minds, and so they cut themselves off from others, either literally or by not seeking their views.

He was as stunned as I was, but didn't put any pressure on me for any particular course of action. In fact I refused to see him over this period as (rightly or wrongly) I didn't want him to be involved.   *Margo*

[It was] my own decision, made automatically. But I also felt my boyfriend did not want a child either. To be fair, I never asked him for his opinion.   *Janice*

When those we care about are happy for us to make the decision by ourselves, they can give us a great deal of support by allowing us real freedom of choice, assuring us that they will support us whether we continue with the pregnancy or have an abortion:

It was left mainly up to me by my husband. I felt that the fact that he had left the decision to me meant that he was not really ready to accept a child. He seemed ready to support me, whatever decision I made. *Vanessa*

My sister and friends are all close to me, the first couple of times I told them. They have all been through it [an unplanned pregnancy] before, so they just said, 'Oh shit, we'll take care of it. You can't, can you?' I said, 'No, I have plans.'   *Glynis*

Others, however, while allowing us to make the decision, only do so because it is what they, for their own reasons, would like us to do. Although the decision is still ours, we can sometimes feel resentful that we are making it so easy for them and that it is we who have to carry all the responsibility.

[It was] my own decision. I was very sensibly and helpfully counselled by my GP who outlined the risks involved with continuing with the pregnancy. My husband was against the pregnancy for his own reasons, but it was my decision alone.   *Joyce*

It was my own decision and [I] was supported by my family and by my boyfriend who said it was my decision – I never had the courage to ask him what he'd do if I said I was going to keep it – I couldn't bear to hear his answer or watch his discomfort. *Rachel*

Sometimes we are forced to make the decision by

ourselves even though we would like to share our feelings
and our fears with others. Our partners may refuse to
discuss it because they are afraid that we may want to
choose a course of action that they do not want; they may
not be prepared to take any responsibility for the decision
as they are afraid they will regret it later on; or they may
be too unsure of the relationship and our feelings for them
to feel they have any right to express an opinion. Not
being able to share the decision-making when we want to
can make us feel very unloved, insecure and lonely.

> All he really said was, 'It's your decision, it's up to
> you.' And I'd say, 'Yes, but what do you really feel?'
> He wouldn't take the responsibility . . . He didn't
> realise that I wanted him to sit down and talk about it,
> but his only real contribution was to say, 'You know
> you could have a mongol child at your age,' which is
> not really what you want to hear . . .   *Betty*

For some of us deciding whether or not to have an
abortion has an important spiritual dimension.
Communicating with our inner spiritual voice, with our
god or goddess or our guides, will be a precious and
necessary part of the decision-making.

Making the decision with others

When we are very close to another person we often want
to share our experience with them. If that person is able
to understand our problems, and is willing to take equal
responsibility, then we can gain a great deal of strength
from their support. Being able to express our deep
feelings and fears and learning about theirs can bring us
very close together and give us a valuable opportunity to
show how much we really care for each other.

> I knew I had to terminate the pregnancy. I was
> supported magnificently by my partner [the baby's
> father] throughout the ensuing grief.   *Katie*

It was a joint decision with my husband. I knew from the start that the decision was what I wanted, but my husband said he would support me if I decided to have a child . . . It did make me feel stronger to have his support.   *Patricia*

Sometimes the person we are closest to – particularly if it is the man with whom we conceived – cannot understand how we feel. Pregnancy is something of which men are often afraid. It is a process they can never experience and is one of the few areas of life over which they have no control. While some men do try to understand how we feel and can by very empathetic, others try to take the decision away from us as a means of re-establishing a position of power.

If we are feeling weak and vulnerable we may not be able to explain or discuss how we feel and what we would like to do, and consequently let them decide. This can result in feelings of bitterness later on because we never made our own choice. Occasionally the pressure is so strong we have an abortion that we do not really want.

[It was] made with my boyfriend – I had very strong pressure from him – I felt pathetically weak at the time and in a way just went along with him as the easiest option – but at the same time I knew this was no cop-out, ultimately it had to be my decision.   *Sheila*

How long we take to decide

Each woman needs a different amount of time in which to make her decision. We may know even before the pregnancy is confirmed that we want to have an abortion, or we may not finally make up our minds until we actually go into the hospital or nursing home for the operation. Some women feel they have never really made a decision, but have allowed circumstances to carry them along. When this happens it is easy to feel powerless and resentful.

> I wanted desperately not to continue to feel I *had* to have an abortion; there was always a feeling on my part that no real decision had been made, it was simply 'out of the question' for me to have a child at that time. *Chris*

Although it is obviously important that we feel as happy as we can about our decision, we also need to bear in mind that the earlier an abortion is performed – preferably before twelve weeks LMP – the safer and less traumatic it is (see *Medical Techniques of Abortion* p 94). If we can make our own decision without suffering any doubts and without ever feeling that we are carrying a potential baby, it is easier for us to come to a decision more quickly:

> I immediately phoned two friends and the father and told them of my absolute decision to have an abortion. The following day I immediately set about procuring the operation. I had absolutely no doubts. *Val*

Second thoughts

Many of us go through a period of doubting our decision, and some of us may decide to continue with the pregnancy. When the doubts are very strong, the decision may have to be made several times:

> I cancelled *two* appointments. *Lorna*

We may also wonder what the baby would be like.

> [I had] momentary doubts only – I thought of the 'romantic' side of having a baby, which occasionally made me doubt if I was doing the right thing. *Rachel*

On a fantasy level I used my pregnancy to find out what my real feelings about motherhood would be. But in my thoughts the baby I would love was always a girl and totally unrelated to the father! If I thought about a boy, then it was like him and I felt revolted by it because of the way he had treated me.   *Liz*

Women who have a strong desire to have a child obviously experience much stronger doubts. Our maternal feelings do not go away just because the time is not right for us to have a baby and we feel deeply upset when we find ourselves in the paradoxical situation of wanting a baby, but knowing it is not right for us to continue with the pregnancy.

Yes, right up to the time of having the abortion I felt it was *wrong* – both morally wrong and also somehow acting against my body's wishes – I actually strongly desire to have a baby – only the circumstances were all wrong.   *Sheila*

Yes. I saw this pregnancy as somehow 'meant to be', as I am rapidly approaching the age when I will no longer be able to conceive.   *Joyce*

Before the abortion, yes I did have doubts. Because I wanted to have a child, but I haven't had doubts since then.   *Jennie*

Our doubts can take the form of guilt. If we do not agree with abortion, either on moral or on religious grounds, we can feel we are violating our principles and may need to give ourselves time to rethink them:

Doubts about the morality of abortion on religious grounds did colour my decision somewhat, but it was a case of 'damned if you do and damned if you don't'. *Marie*

Some women feel they are committing murder:

It felt like murder, and it went against my principles as a person and also as a professional. It was, however, the only reasonable decision for us to make as a couple.   *Katie*

Some feel guilty because they do not feel their reasons for abortion are 'good enough'. Society continually devalues the motivation of women and we may not have sufficient confidence in ourselves to accept that our reasons are perfectly valid.

Financially there would be no reason why we couldn't have a child, my husband has secure employment and we have our own home. I have dealt with parents unable to conceive and so felt guilty.   *Patricia*

Our decision can seem to be a form of weakness and we blame ourselves for getting pregnant in the first place and then again for deciding to have an abortion:

Yes I doubted all the time. I thought it was a coward's way out. It was my fault I got pregnant, I never liked the idea of abortion, I think I believe it's a form of murder.   *Janet*

Sometimes our guilt emerges as the fear that if we have an abortion we shall be punished. Or we feel that we shall always be made to regret what we have done.

Of course I had doubts, I think everybody does. Mainly I wondered if I would regret my decision, though I never have.   *Vanessa*

All of these feelings are normal and don't necessarily mean we have made the wrong decision. Nevertheless they should not be denied or suppressed. Talk them through with someone close to you or with an abortion counsellor.

The Laws

England, Wales and Scotland

The three laws that operate in England and Wales and which determine if it is legal for a doctor to perform an abortion are: the Offences Against the Person Act 1861, the Infant Life (Preservation) Act 1929, and the Abortion Act 1967. In Scotland only the Abortion Act 1967 applies.[6] In this section these laws are looked at in terms of the conditions we have to satisfy in order to obtain a legal abortion.

Since the Abortion Act 1967 came into effect on 27 April 1968, an abortion can be performed legally if two medical practitioners agree that one of the following conditions applies to the woman requesting a termination, if the pregnancy is terminated by a registered medical practitioner, and is performed, other than in an emergency, in a National Health Service hospital or in a approved place:

(a) the continuance of the pregnancy would involve risk to the life of the pregnant woman greater than if the pregnancy were terminated;
(b) the termination is necessary to prevent grave permanent injury to the physical or mental health of the pregnant woman;
(c) the continuance of the pregnancy would involve risk of injury to the physical or mental health of the pregnant woman greater than if the pregnancy were terminated;
(d) the continuance of the pregnancy would involve risk of injury to the physical or mental health of any existing child(ren) greater than if the pregnancy were terminated;
(e) there is a substantial risk that if the child were born it would suffer from such physical or mental

abnormalities as to be seriously disabled
or, in an emergency, certified by the operating practitioner as being immediately necessary;
(f) to save the life of the pregnant woman; and
(g) to prevent permanent injury to the physical or mental
health of the pregnant woman.

In deciding whether you qualify under any of these
clauses, doctors are allowed to take into account your
present or reasonably foreseeable circumstances. This is
known as 'the social clause' and takes into account your
financial, home and marital circumstances, etc.

The 1995 abortion statistics for England and Wales,
issued by the Office for National Statistics, revealed that
90 per cent of all abortions were performed under clause
(c), 8 per cent under clause (d), 1.4 per cent under clause
(b), 1.1 per cent under clause (e), and only .09 per cent
under clause (a).[7] Since all terminations carried out in the
first 12 weeks of pregnancy carry a far lower risk than
childbirth itself, it could be argued that *all* first trimester
abortions are legal under clause (c) of the Act.

Time limit

The Abortion Act 1967 was amended in 1990 by Section
37 of the Human Fertilisation and Embryology Act. The
main change is that there is now an upper time limit of
24 weeks for legal abortion (previously 28 weeks). There
is no upper time limit in extreme cases under clauses (a),
(d) and (f).

Age of consent

If you are under 16 you normally need the consent of a
parent, guardian or person acting in *loco parentis* before
an abortion can be performed. However, the law does
say that a girl under 16 can consent to her own treatment

if her doctor considers her to be mature enough to make the decision. But few doctors are prepared to give medical treatment under these circumstances. The best thing to do in this situation is to contact one of the agencies such as the British Pregnancy Advisory Service listed in the Resources Section. They will be sympathetic and can provide practical advice and support.

Performing your own abortion

It is illegal to attempt to perform an abortion by yourself with the help of a friend, or a women's group. The 1967 Act states that an abortion has to be carried out by a *registered medical practitioner*, while the Offences Against the Person Act 1861 states that any woman who is pregnant and who *administers to herself any poison or other noxious thing* with intent to procure her own miscarriage, or *unlawfully uses any instrument or other means whatsoever* for the same intent, is liable to prosecution and life imprisonment. Similarly, any person who helps her is likely to suffer heavy penalties. As late as 1978, the Director of Public Prosecutions considered prosecuting a young woman under 16 and her 16-year-old brother after she had taken laxative chocolate which he had bought, and had sat in a hot bath in an attempt to abort her pregnancy.

Conscientious objection

Any doctor, nurse or other person involved in the termination of a pregnancy can lawfully refuse to help if they give conscientious objection as a reason. Under the 1967 Act no person has a duty to participate *whether by contract or by any statutory or legal requirement* in any treatment relating to procuring an abortion unless the woman needs an abortion in order to save her life, or if not having an abortion would result in grave permanent injury to her physical or mental health.

Northern Ireland

The 1967 and 1929 Acts do not apply in Northern Ireland, although the 1861 Act does. The Criminal Justice Act (Northern Ireland) 1945[8] permits abortion under the following conditions:

(a) a serious medical or psychological problem exists which means childbirth would jeopardise a woman's life;
(b) the woman is mentally handicapped;
(c) the woman can prove she has been in contact with rubella (German measles) in early pregnancy; and
(d) there is a substantial genetic risk of a mentally handicapped child.

Even under this law many doctors still refuse to perform an abortion, and women claiming grounds under the psychological clause frequently have to cope with the stress and indignity of persuading two psychiatrists to ratify their claim. Significantly, rape is not considered a legal condition for termination of pregnancy.

Irish Republic

In the Republic abortion is illegal under any conditions; and in 1983 its illegality was written into the Constitution after a referendum was held on whether it should be made part of the Constitution to give the unborn child the same rights as the mother. A majority of those voting – although not a majority of the population – supported the amendment. In its most inhumane interpretation, this can allow a doctor to refuse to perform an abortion even though it is necessary to ensure the good health of the mother.

However, in 1992 an amendment guaranteed the right to travel abroad for an abortion, the right to information on abortion, and the right to an abortion when a pregnancy threatens the life but not the health of the pregnant woman. Health advisors can provide information on the options (adoption, fostering, termination, etc) and must put equal emphasis on each option.

The procedure

In order to obtain a legal abortion, two forms have to be signed by registered medical practitioners. In England and Wales these are the form HSA 1 and form HSA 4.

Form HSA 1

Form HSA 1, which sets out the clauses under which an abortion can legally be performed, must be signed by two doctors who consider *in good faith* that you fall within the terms of the 1967 Act before an abortion can be carried out. If you have a sympathetic GP who agrees to refer you for an abortion, then she or he normally provides the first signature, the second signature being provided by the doctor who sees you at the hospital, abortion charity or private organisation. The second doctor may or may not be the doctor who performs the operation.

If your GP has a supply of form HSA 1 in the surgery then she or he should either give you one with a letter of referral for you to pass on to the second doctor, or post one to the hospital on your behalf. In some areas of the country GPs do not have a supply of the form, in which case if they agree you have grounds for a termination you will be given a letter of referral to the hospital. If the hospital doctor agrees with your GP then she or he will sign the form which you will then have to take back to your GP for signature, and return it to the hospital before your operation.

If your GP will not sign the form, but has referred you to an NHS hospital, then two doctors at the hospital –

provided that they agree that you qualify under the 1967 Act – will provide the two signatures. One will normally be the gynaecologist who sees you, the other the admitting doctor who checks you are physically fit to have an operation. This may be the doctor who performs the operation, who can sign the form provided she or he has seen you before the operation.

Should you not want to involve your GP and can self-refer to an NHS day-care unit (not all these units accept self-referrals), abortion charity or private organisation, then form HSA 1 will be signed by two doctors at the unit or the organisation's offices. Doctors at the Brook Clinics and some family planning clinics will also sign.

After the abortion is performed form HSA 1 is taken from your notes and sent to the Chief Medical Officer, Department of Health.

Form HSA 4

Only the doctor who operates has to fill in form HSA 4. This is very detailed, requiring the operating doctor's name and qualifications, your name, address, marital status, period of gestation, history of past pregnancies, including live births, stillbirths, spontaneous miscarriages and terminations, method of abortion, the clause under which the abortion is deemed legal, and any complications experienced while you are at the hospital.

As with Form HSA 1, Form HSA 4 is sent to the Department of Health after the termination.

The role of the GP

The GP's attitude is an important factor in determining not only how we feel about our decision to have an abortion but also, since GPs have the power of referral, in whether we can obtain an NHS abortion or have to go to the charitable or private sector. Many GPs are very helpful, do everything they can to refer us to a sympathetic gynaecologist, and offer us a non-directive counselling service, if that is what we want. If they know there is likely to be a long waiting list at the hospital they will explain the implications of this and find out if we can afford to have an abortion performed by one of the abortion charities.

Other GPs however can be obstructive or unhelpful. Unfortunately there is no list available which lets us know if our GP is pro-choice or not, and we only find out what his/her attitude is when we ask for help. Often we go in expecting and prepared to be confronted with a negative attitude. The number of women who express surprise at being treated well is a depressing indication of the strength of a vocal section of society that still condemns our fundamental, if not legal, right to make our own decision:

> The doctor was incredibly nice and I was quite surprised because I knew other women who've had horrendous times with the NHS. I was just very lucky I guess. *Sandra*

What we need from our GP will vary from woman to woman. Some of us just want a letter of referral – 'He actively helped – I didn't go for advice but to be referred to hospital' *Ros* – while others want emotional support and information on practical and medical procedures:

> I saw a local GP (my own GP was in Bath where I had been living). He was wonderful, very kind and sympathetic and, once he had realised that I definitely wanted an abortion, he set all the wheels rolling very quickly. He seemed to go out of his way to help me. *Alice*

Sometimes GPs may be willing to refer us, but refuse to give the other support we need, making us feel we are unworthy of their time and concern:

My GP showed less interest in my request for an abortion than she did in my cold sores! She wrote me a referral letter, but never asked how I felt or offered any information. *I* had ask *her* what the delays at the hospital were. She just said, 'Why don't you ring and ask them?' I said, 'What if there is a really long waiting list? I can't cope with being pregnant for much longer, it's upsetting me too much.' And she said, 'Go private. You probably won't get one on the NHS, you weren't using contraception.' I felt like crying, I changed to a different doctor after that.   *Liz*

The majority of GPs are white, middle-class and often find it difficult to understand women who come from a background different from their own, Some try to empathise, but others make assumptions based on the dominant viewpoint of their own culture.

As worrying, is the tendency of some doctors to try to persuade women to have an abortion because they are not English or are working-class on the grounds that she or he doesn't believe they would make good mothers or a belief that they should be discouraged from reproducing for eugenic reasons. A few doctors take these assumptions to extremes and strongly recommend to the woman or gynaecologist that a sterilisation or IUD fitting should be carried out at the same time as the abortion.

Some GPs can also find it impossible to understand why a married woman would want to have an abortion:

He agreed to the abortion only after I informed him that my husband and I were separated. . . On learning of my separation he agreed to give his consent because it was 'another man's baby'.   *Chris*

He was fairly sympathetic but only because I had been in a stable marriage for ten years and it was just 'bad luck'. He did say he'd be less supportive if it happened again . . .   *Cheryl*

Sometimes the only way to get a GP to help us is to fight persistently against his/her arguments, an effort which some of us may feel too weak and vulnerable to make:

> He reacted with total disbelief that I wouldn't want to continue with the pregnancy. He treated it as a matter of course that although it was contraceptive failure it would be all right 'once you've got the baby in your arms'.   *Patricia*

Other doctors refuse to help us either subtly by postponing the issue or by suggesting we try outside the NHS, or directly, by saying no:

> My GP told me that the hospital gynaecologist was not very sympathetic and that he was hesitant about referring too many cases to the gynaecologist. However I got a very strong impression that my GP was disapproving and trying to put me off.   *Margo*

When a GP is unhelpful

Make your own appointment

If you feel that your GP really does not want to help you, even though she or he has promised to make an appointment for you at the clinic or hospital, then insist that you take the letter of referral yourself and make your own appointment. It is not unknown for doctors to say that they will make an appointment and not do so, or to delay making it for so long that the type of abortion you eventually have performed is more traumatic.

> It took too damn long, nearly three weeks between the first appointment with the GP and the consultant. My

GP apparently 'forgot' to make an appointment.
Chris

Alternative action

The British Medical Association guidelines state that
doctors 'have a duty to assist the patient to obtain
alternative medical advice', however it does not say what
form this medical advice should take. Some doctors will
suggest you contact another GP who they know is
sympathetic, while others offer little real assistance,
avoiding the issue by suggesting you ring an abortion
charity or other organisation.

Even if your GP is totally unhelpful, there are several
courses of action open to you.

Changing GPs

If there is more than one doctor in the practice then it is
worth asking if there is a GP there who is pro-choice.
Changing practices is not a good idea, unless you are
certain the doctor to whom you are trying to transfer is
sympathetic to abortion, as it can be a time-consuming
procedure so that the chances of your having to have a
late abortion increase. If a friend has a pro-choice doctor
you can try registering as a temporary patient, saying you
are on holiday and using the address of your friend.

Brook Advisory Centres

Brook Advisory Centres (see pp 183–5 for details) can
refer you to a gynaecologist without the consent of your
GP. Appointments can be made by phone. The Brook
keep special slots in their appointment books for women
who believe they may be pregnant, and will always try to
see them immediately. If the urine test is positive you will
see one of their doctors who will discuss the pregnancy
with you and who will, if you wish to have a
termination, determine under which clause of the Act

you qualify for a legal abortion. Wherever possible the Brook refer women to an NHS hospital. Brook Advisory Centres also do everything they can to try to counsel in the first language of the woman.

Family planning clinics

Only a few family planning clinics are able to refer you for an NHS abortion, so it is always advisable to ring them first to check whether they are able to offer this service.

Abortion charities

If you live in an area where very few abortions are performed under the NHS, then any doctor, however helpful, will have difficulty arranging an NHS abortion. If this applies to you, or if you do not want to fight, or wait, for an NHS operation and can afford to pay for an abortion, one of the easiest and least traumatic routes is to go to the British Pregnancy Advisory Service which performs abortions in its own clinics (see pp 179–80 for details). You do not need a referral from your doctor, nor will she or he be informed of your visit to the charity without your consent.

In addition there are some charitable pregnancy advisory services, such as Marie Stopes House in London, authorised to sign the form HSA 1 and provide all the testing and counselling services involved in the process of obtaining an abortion. These organisations do not always have their own operating facilities and may therefore refer you to Department of Health approved clinics.

Private organisations and clinics

There are a number of private pregnancy advisory bureaux registered by the Department of Health under the 1967 Act which can arrange for you to have a legal abortion at an approved clinic. Some of these provide a very good service at a cost similar to those charged by the charities; others are more expensive, however. There are also a few registered clinics under the Act which advertise abortion provision in Yellow Pages and women's magazines. With both the clinics and the pregnancy bureaux it is advisable to ring before making an appointment to establish what the fees are and whether counselling and after-care services are included.

Ireland

If you live in Ireland and know that your GP is unsympathetic to abortion then you are unlikely to seek help from her or him in any form. Unless a woman can give an address in England, it is difficult to obtain an NHS abortion so the majority of Irish women have their abortions performed either at the abortion charities or in private clinics.

In Northern Ireland the Ulster Pregnancy Advisory Service, and some family planning clinics and women's groups will help women book an appointment at a clinic in London, Liverpool or Birmingham. Likewise, the Well Woman Centres and some family planning clinics offer this service to women in the Republic. These organisations may contact the Irish Women's Support Group in London or the Liverpool Support Service who liaise with BPAS, meet women and take them to the clinics, generally explain the procedures to them, and ensure their safe return.

NHS or non-NHS?

In 1995 the National Health Service performed 54.7 per cent of all operations carried out on residents in England and Wales, and paid for a further 15.8 per cent to be undertaken in private clinics under agency agreements.[9] The remainder were carried out by abortion charities and registered pregnancy advisory bureaux. In Scotland, where there is only a very small private sector, 95.9 per cent of abortions were carried out under the NHS in 1994, and 363 women travelled to England to have abortions.[10]

The extent to which we can choose between the services will depend initially on whether we can pay for an abortion outside the NHS, and secondly, on whether the abortion provision in the area in which we live is such that an NHS abortion is a possibility. In cases when a termination is necessary to save the life of a woman, or in cases of foetal abnormality, an abortion can nearly always be obtained on the NHS.

Women have good and bad experiences both within the NHS and outside of it. Consequently it would be misleading to make sweeping generalisations which condemn one service while applauding another. Significant differences between the services do exist, however, which may effect our choice of where we want to have our abortion performed.

National Health Service

Geographical disparity

In 1995 four health regions performed less than the NHS national average of 54.7 per cent of all abortions performed. These were the West Midlands, which performed only 19.6 per cent of abortions in its catchment area; South Thames, 42.3 per cent; North Thames, 49 per cent; and North West England, 54.1 per cent. Each of these areas also had agency agreements, West Midlands paying for 7620 abortions to be carried out in private clinics.[11]

Some abortion campaigners believe that the increasing number of abortions being paid for by the NHS but carried out by specialist private clinics is an encouraging trend. There are advantages to women being treated in specialist units, with staff employed specifically to provide an abortion service.

A Royal Commission on the NHS in 1979 recommended that the NHS should undertake 75 per cent of all abortions, and that regional differences should be ironed out. NHS abortions are becoming easier to get, but most regions of Britain still trail behind the Royal Commission target.

Delays

The delays faced by some women when trying to get an NHS abortion are well documented. In *Late Abortions in England and Wales* (1984), a comprehensive study of more than 9000 cases, the Royal College of Obstetricians and Gynaecologists revealed that 20 per cent of women who had their operations between 20 and 23 weeks' gestation and nearly 40 per cent of those having abortions at 15 to 16 weeks had been referred by doctors *before* the end of the 12th week of pregnancy.[12]

A survey carried out by the Birth Control Trust in 1995 showed that delays are still a considerable problem. More than a third of the abortion providers in the survey said there was an interval of more than two weeks between referral and abortion, and in three instances there was a delay of one month.[13]

Such a delay often leads those women who can afford it to seek help outside the NHS before the 12th week in order to avoid having a later operation which is more traumatic, both in terms of the waiting time and the type of operation which is carried out.

> When I rang the hospital for an appointment the receptionist said there was a two-week waiting list for an appointment. I asked how long after the appointment would it be before I could get an abortion. She told me . . . that it could be anything from three to four weeks. I rang the BPAS immediately, even though I couldn't really afford it.   *Liz*

Delays may occur for many reasons, one of which may be the unhelpful attitude of the booking clerk. In *Abortion Services in London*, a survey of 31 health authorities in the Greater London Council area carried out in 1984 by Women's Health researchers discovered that 'Booking clerks have immense power and can cause a great deal of distress by knowingly booking women with unsympathetic gynaecologists.[14] Other causes for delay are the lack of gynaecologists willing to perform abortions, and insufficient operating hours available for this operation.

Abortion techniques

There are marked differences between the choices of abortion method used in NHS and private hospitals. These become more significant the later the gestational age. Under twelve weeks' gestation, vacuum suction is used almost equally by both sectors. After this period vaginal procedures (vacuum aspiration, dilation and curettage, dilation and evacuation – see p.00 for an explanation of procedures) tend to be more commonly used outside the NHS and over a wider range of gestational ages. Between 13 and 19 weeks of pregnancy, 54 per cent of abortions were performed vaginally outside the NHS while only 10 per cent such operations were performed in the NHS, an induced abortion generally being the preferred method within the NHS, at this stage.[15]

When there is a waiting list of three or four weeks, this method preference can result in a situation where a woman who has been accepted for an abortion at 11 weeks LMP has to wait until 15 weeks LMP for an induced abortion when a simple vacuum suction abortion, possibly combined with D & C or D & E, could have been carried out earlier.

The BPAS

The British Pregnancy Advisory Service was founded in 1968 after the passing of the Abortion Act when it was recognised that the NHS would be unable to meet the need for abortion advice and treatment. The BPAS is a registered charity and is non-profit-making.

BPAS was founded in Birmingham in response to the difficulties created by consultant gynaecologists in that area who expressed a conscientious objection to abortion. Since that time it has opened 30 further branches, the majority of which have been registered by the Department of Health as pregnancy advisory bureaux under the Abortion Act 1967, and owns nine clinics all approved by the Department of Health under the terms of the 1967 Act.

BPAS pioneered day-care units and offers a wide range of services apart from pregnancy testing and abortion, including contraception, post-coital contraception, sterilisation, vasectomy and counselling.

BPAS is not subject to the same financial restrictions as the NHS and can therefore generally provide a quicker and more sympathetic service. Women who are resident in England, Wales and Scotland, are having first trimester abortions (those carried out before 12 weeks LMP) and who live within two hours' travelling time of the clinic, may have their abortions carried out on a day-care basis as long as they are met by a friend and do not spend the first night after the operation alone.

BPAS gives detailed information about abortion techniques and provides empathetic counselling by non-medical staff who are not therefore involved in the authorisation of referrals. Most of their counsellors are women and you do not have to see a male counsellor if you are unhappy to do so. They do everything they can to help disabled women, and will arrange consultations if access to their premises is difficult for those with limited mobility.

Private clinics

Some private clinics perform a very good and inexpensive service. If there is one in your area which is nearer than a BPAS clinic then you may find it more convenient to have your abortion performed there.

The consultation

Whether we have an abortion at an NHS hospital or in the charitable or private sector, we normally have to go through a consultation which entails a number of routine procedures. These include getting a second (in some cases first and second) signature on form HSA 1; a physical examination; blood test and review of our medical history to determine that we are physically fit to have an operation; and a vaginal examination to assess the size of the uterus and thereby the number of weeks' gestation. We are also normally given a pregnancy test and may be given counselling and advice on contraception.

The extent to which we shall have to explain our reasons for wanting an abortion to the doctor will depend on how much information she or he already has about us. If we have seen a counsellor before the consultation, or if our GP has presented our reasons clearly and in depth in the referral letter, then we may not have to answer many questions apart from those which relate to our medical history. If the doctor does not have this information then we may be asked to answer a number of personal questions about why we want an abortion. Obviously the extent to which we feel able to do this happily will depend on the attitude of the doctor. Sensitive and sympathetic doctors can make us feel positive:

The consultant was male, all the other doctors were female. They were all very sympathetic and gentle – at no time did I feel I had to become hysterical in order to get an abortion.   *Alice*

I only saw the consultant, who was sympathetic, but questioned my initial feelings, those of my husband and future plans for children. He was realistic, but did not make me feel as though I should be ashamed. *Patricia*

Other doctors are more judgemental, putting us in a negative position where we not only have to justify our reasons, but may actually be called upon to argue against their prejudices.

The male consultant treated me with contempt. His wife had just had her third baby that day so he was into being a father. He could not understand *why* I should want an abortion, being married with only one child, and suggested that perhaps my husband was not the father!   *Cheryl*

The consultant gynaecologist at the hospital was offensive, rude and obviously anti-abortion, although he did consent to the termination on the grounds that if he didn't, 'She'd only go off and pay £100 for it elsewhere.'   *Chris*

If, after having interviewed us, the gynaecologist refuses to give her or his consent, we should ask to be referred to another consultant who is more sympathetic to abortion. If the doctor agrees to this, insist an appointment is made *before* you leave so that you know what the delay is likely to be. If there is a long delay, or if you are unsure of the views of the second gynaecologist, it is advisable to book an appointment with one of the abortion charities.

In certain hospitals and private clinics in Northern Ireland some women have to face the humiliation and degradation of convincing two psychiatrists that their mental health is such that they are unable to have a child. This was the case in Britain before the 1967 Act.

> The psychiatrist tried to make me say I really wanted another baby and that was why I had become pregnant. That was, of course, rubbish. I had to be very dramatic – tears and all – to convince him that this wasn't the case, that I might do myself in if I had to go through with it – although that part was untrue – that it would be totally unfair on the boys and me to have it, etc. All very upsetting.   *Barbara*

Medical examination

You will be asked a number of questions about your past health and will probably have a blood sample taken. If this reveals that you are anaemic you will be prescribed a course of iron tablets to take before the operation, as all abortions involve some blood loss which can make you feel tired and depressed if you are already suffering from anaemia.

The vaginal examination is carried out bimanually. The gynaecologist inserts the index and middle fingers of one hand into the vagina and uses the other hand to palpate the lower abdominal wall. This allows the doctor to feel the size, shape, mobility and position of the uterus, Fallopian tubes and ovaries, and will locate any unusual growths, pelvic pain, or other abnormalities. There may be a little discomfort felt when she or he touches the ovaries and it helps if you can relax.

The gynaecologist may also want to look at the cervix to see whether any infection is present. This involves the insertion of a speculum to open up the vaginal walls so that the doctor can get a clear view. Having an internal examination is rarely pleasant and when we are pregnant this examination may be particularly upsetting, so the gentleness of the doctor is all-important.

He was wonderful, very gentle and reassuring, he told me what he was going to do and apologised for having to be intrusive. This, coupled with his anger at the way my boyfriend had deserted me, made me want to cry. I thought, 'Not all men are bastards.'   *Liz*

When the doctor is brutal or judgemental, the experience can be like a sexual assault:

I felt like I was being raped when he did the internal, he made it so obvious that he found me and my request disgusting.   *Chris*

Most methods of abortions involve instruments being passed through the cervix and into the uterus. Consequently if there is any infection present in the vagina, it will be spread upwards at the time of the abortion. So if you have a history of genital, pelvic or tubal infection, have a heavy discharge, feel some pain, or believe that you may have an infection at the time of requesting an abortion, it is very important that you tell the doctor. It is a good idea to ask to be screened for chlamydia when you have your pre-abortion examination. Chlamdia is the most common sexually transmitted disease in Britain. The majority of women who are infected don't know they have it. If it spreads into your uterus, fallopian tubes or ovaries it can cause a serious infection called pelvic inflammatory disease which may lead to infertility. If caught early the treatment is simple – a single dose of antibiotics will clear up the infection very quickly. Your partner(s) must also be tested and given treatment, otherwise you will be re-infected.

The other main types of infection which can cause severe infection are gonorrhoea and syphyllis (VD). If any infection is present it can be treated pre-operatively. *It does not mean that you will be refused an abortion*. As screening is expensive it is not always carried out as a routine, although the BPAS always screens for gonorrhoea and syphyllis, and will test for chlamdia if an internal examination or past history indicates infection may be present.

Pregnancy counselling

Pregnancy counselling is often a major part of the consultation process and, depending on where we have our abortion performed, it may be carried out by a trained lay worker, social worker, the doctor who agrees that we qualify for an abortion under the terms and conditions of the Abortion Act, or by another doctor. It may take place before we see a referring doctor or afterwards.

There has been much discussion within the NHS and elsewhere about the form that counselling should take, what it should involve, and the attributes that a good counsellor needs in order to be of most use to women who wish to have an abortion. There is general agreement that counselling should take place in private, be non-directive and non-judgemental in its approach, that counsellors should be empathetic, exhibit non-possessive warmth, be open-minded, attentive and able to listen, and that they should discuss the practical aspects of abortion as well as the emotional ones. In some cases counselling will also involve a discussion of contraception and the woman's attitude to future methods of birth control. At its best counselling should help us to make our own decision about the pregnancy, based on a realistic understanding of ourselves and our circumstances, help us to avoid another unwanted pregnancy and leave us feeling informed and confident about the operation. The counsellor will normally want to see us on our own first, although she or he will see other people connected with us and our decision if we request it. The counsellor may also want to see them if it appears that we are being pressured into taking a course of action we are not happy about.

> The female counsellor was great, not judgemental. (I had a dread of being 'ticked off'.) She was just anxious to make sure that I wasn't being pressured into any particular course of action by other people.   *Margo*

> The counsellor was a social worker, that was quite obvious. She was very pleasant towards me and talked the whole thing through. She certainly did not try to change my outlook, but simply tried to assure a termination of pregnancy was what I wanted. *Vanessa*

For some of us, the stage at which the counselling takes place is crucial to the benefit we can derive from it. If we are undecided about whether we want an abortion or not, or feel we are being forced into having a termination, then it is obviously more helpful for us to see a counsellor who can help us to come to the right decision before we see a doctor.

On the other hand, seeing a counsellor first, particularly if we have decided we want an abortion, can appear like a test which we have to pass in order to qualify. Fear of saying the 'wrong' thing can prevent us from discussing any worries or misgivings we have, and consequently deprive us of an opportunity for reassurance and support. When we are being counselled by one of the referring doctors we are even less likely to be open, unless the doctor agrees to an abortion before discussing our emotional feelings.

> On the whole she was very good, but even though I knew the BPAS would probably give me an abortion, there was still an irrational fear that I might not qualify. So I wasn't as honest as I would have liked to have been . . . I cut myself off from an opportunity to be helped.   *Liz*

When our pregnancy is the outcome, rather than the cause, of emotional crisis, then the counsellor may try to discover what the underlying problem is in an effort to help us sort out our lives in general.

Sometimes the reason for our becoming pregnant is so painful that we reject any offer of help and pretend we are fine. Admitting to having a serious problem in our life is never easy, and when we are feeling confused and vulnerable we often do not feel safe or confident enough to face up to the fact that we are unloved and unrecognised by our husbands, lovers, children or parents, or that we feel a failure in our working lives. We may feel too guilty to explain that our pregnancy was the only way we could get attention of any kind because we are afraid such a reason would not be treated with respect or understanding. Yet often, if we can begin to discuss these issues, a good counsellor will be able to help us find ways of solving them.

> Perhaps if I'd talked then, I could have saved myself three years of wondering who I was, why I was so depressed most of the time and why I was so angry. *Liz*

> It's happening again – 'I'd like to get pregnant now' – and it's like I want to scream, 'For God's sake, someone slap me around the face and stop me having this passive attitude to it, you know you have got control and you can stop it.'   *Sandra*

We can also find it difficult to express how we feel if English is not our first language. But even when English is our first language, culture or class differences between us and the counsellor can be a barrier to real understanding.

> Quite possibly white people don't want black women to have children now they are not 'required' or

'squired' for slavery. It is an insidious form of racism.
Lorna

Very occasionally we see a counsellor who is totally unsuitable for the job she or he is doing.

The female counsellor was very unpleasant. Tried to get me to break down and cry for about half an hour. Told me, 'It's *not* abortion on demand you know.' It seemed like you didn't have sufficient grounds unless you cracked up and got extremely distressed in her office.   *Cath*

One of the counsellor's roles is to give practical support, such as discussing how we are going to take time off if we are working, suggesting we book a babysitter in advance, arrange for someone to collect us from the hospital or clinic and stay with us after the operation, reminding us of what we shall need to take with us, etc. These details may seem mundane, but it is easy to forget them when so much else is going on in our lives.

Contraceptive advice

Most doctors feel that women who are seeking an abortion should be given advice about contraception, and be encouraged to accept a particular method at some stage during the consultation, either when the woman sees the doctor or when she speaks to the counsellor. Whether this is the best possible time for advice to be given is difficult to determine. Some of us find it very helpful because our confidence in the method we have been using has been undermined and we are anxious to know what else we can use. Others find it an intrusion: we haven't asked for the information and feel that being made to think about birth control at this stage is either inappropriate or implies that the doctor believes the pregnancy has been caused by our carelessness.

Generally speaking, those of us who welcome the advice given at this time, or are not upset by it, are those who are treated with understanding by the doctor, who are encouraged to talk openly about any past contraceptive problems, and who are not coerced into accepting a particular method:

She explained all the contraceptives clearly and how they are used. I found it very helpful as I then knew what to use afterwards. It didn't bother me at this stage at all, I was just grateful for the detailed advice. *Sally*

In contrast, if we feel we are being blamed for not using contraception, or that we, and not the method we have been using, is being held responsible for our pregnancy, then we are unlikely to retain any advice we are given. We may feel angry, hurt or guilty:

I was advised that it would be better to start an oral contraceptive. I did not feel it appropriate to discuss future contraception and certainly didn't retain the advice.   *Patricia*

I showed her the triphasic pills I had been waiting to take when my periods started. She didn't listen, just kept on about 'fixing me up with a cap'. I'm sure her insistence stemmed from concern, but it made me feel I was not to be trusted.   *Liz*

[I was] pressured to take the pill. I told them I shouldn't because of a family history of thrombosis, but they were very insistent . . .   *Cath*

For lesbians the suggestion that they should use contraception regularly is not only out of place, but is yet another occasion when they are forced to confront society's unwillingness to accept their sexuality.

. . . in hospital the word 'lesbian' was on my medical

forms, yet the doctors seemed incapable of understanding it or pronouncing it – preferring to conceal it beneath a sales drive on spermicides and rubber technology.   *Ros*

Occasionally doctors will only agree to consent to an abortion if the woman has an IUD or is sterilised at the same time. The minority of doctors who take this inhuman stance are those who do not accept that a woman has any status at all, and therefore believe she is incapable of controlling her own fertility. Class and race prejudices often determine that it is working-class and black women who already have children who are put in this position.

If a doctor tries to insist on either of these measures, or suggests we should comply with them, we should refuse and ask to see another doctor, not only because having an IUD inserted, or being sterilised at the same time as abortion increases the risks attached to the operation but also because our bodies are our own and no one has the right to try to coerce us into acquiescing to their abuse. IUDs inserted at the same time as an abortion can lead to prolonged bleeding, pain and sometimes infection. This may not be explained to us and, if we are feeling vulnerable, it is only to easy to agree. (See pp 113–14 for the increased risk of having an IUD inserted or sterilisation combined with an abortion.)

No advice [was offered] but I would have liked some because I could not take the pill because of a physical reaction and I didn't really know what to use because of the failure of the diaphragm. A coil was suggested when I went to the hospital, just before the abortion. I *think* it was offered as an option, but as I said I would try it, I didn't really test them out.   *Janice*

While it may be wrong to pressure a woman to have an IUD inserted, it is barbaric to encourage her to be sterilised. Sterilisation can be irreversible and therefore we need to feel secure and positive when we decide whether we wish to take such a major step. Just before an abortion, when we are under a considerable amount of stress, and have a limited amount of time, is not the right moment, and a wise doctor will suggest we do not consider it until afterwards.

Support

As the consultation can be physically and emotionally stressful, it can help if we have someone with us to give us support, particularly if we are very nervous or tearful. For women who cannot speak English it is essential to have someone who can interpret.

> My husband stayed in the waiting room, but I felt that we were going through the anguish together. He felt that he needed to come with me and I needed to support him.   *Patricia*

> My tutor warden came with me, and it was easier with her there, because we had talked about it beforehand, so I knew what to expect.   *Sally*

> [It was] very comforting. Although I didn't communicate, it was good to have someone there who would listen if I wanted to talk.   *Marie*

Some women are very happy to go on their own, but others, especially if they are treated unkindly, can feel terrified and isolated.

> No one came. The experience was horrific. It lasted about three hours in all, with the waiting and everything. I sincerely wish I'd had a strong, supportive woman friend with me.   *Chris*

> I was terrified by the whole experience. I felt outclassed by things like little machines on doors that

spoke to you (I had to have it explained to me as I waited on the doorstep). I was not yet 21 and was very anxious about the illegality being discovered, i.e. if I died on the operating table.   *Nell*

Waiting

After we have been accepted for an abortion we normally have to wait anything from a few days to several weeks before we are admitted to a hospital or clinic for the operation. In general the delay is likely to be longer in the NHS than in the charitable or private sector. It is important that we take care of ourselves during this period, making sure we have enough rest, trying to eat well and letting ourselves be loved by those who care for us.

3
Having an Abortion

> I was incredibly relieved when I knew I was no longer pregnant. I went to the bathroom and looked at myself in the mirror and I felt like I was seeing myself again for the first time in ages. I sort of welcomed myself back into myself. It was a great feeling. *Liz*

The way we feel just before, during and after a termination varies enormously. Some of us feel very positive throughout this period and are impatient for the operation to be performed, while others experience feelings of worthlessness, panic, fear and numbness.

Since an abortion can be a deeply emotional and spiritual experience as well as a physical one, the way we react to the operation will depend very much on how happy we are with the course of action we have chosen. If we know that what we are doing is right for us, and have been supported by people we trust, then we feel stronger and less anxious than if the decision has been made for us, or if we have been forced into it by others or by circumstances beyond our control. For those with religious or spiritual beliefs, it may be important to 'say goodbye' to the potential life inside us, committing it back to the spiritual world in which we believe.

The way we feel will also be affected by how much information we have been given about the operation – what it involves, what risks there are, and how we can expect to feel afterwards. Any operation, however minor, is potentially frightening because it is something over which we have little direct control. The more we know about the surgical procedure, therefore, the less likely we are to experience irrational fears and worries. For this reason this chapter contains quite detailed accounts of all the procedures involved in different types of abortion.

Medical techniques of abortion

Different medical techniques are used to terminate a pregnancy depending on the stage of gestation. In the first stages of pregnancy a fertilised egg attaches itself to the lining of the uterus about seven days after conception has taken place and starts to grow.

About four weeks after conception (around six weeks LMP) the embryo is a pea-sized mass of tissue. Eight weeks from conception, the embryo has grown to about 1 inch in length and has begun to take on human shape. At this stage it is usually referred to as a foetus rather than an embryo. Twelve weeks after conception it is about three inches long and a fluid-filled sac, known as the amniotic sac, has grown around it. The foetus is fed by the placenta. The heartbeat can be detected with a sonic aid from 11 weeks or so and foetal movements usually start between 18 and 22 weeks.

When an abortion is performed, the contents of the uterus, which include the foetus, the placenta and tissue which has built up on the lining of the uterus, are removed.

An abortion, particularly when carried out in the first 12 weeks, is an extremely safe operation. Since the Abortion Act 1967 came into effect, medical techniques have evolved rapidly and there has been a significant decrease in both the mortality (death) and morbidity (complications) rates. Abortions performed in the first 12 weeks of pregnancy carry a mortality rate of less than 1 in 200,000. In England and Wales, between 1977 and 1991 only 32 deaths were recorded as resulting from abortion.[1]

The risk of complications is also very low. In 1995 only 0.4 per cent of abortions performed in the first trimester resulted in any complications during the hospital stay, any complications arising after the hospital stay being minor and responding quickly to simple treatment by a GP. The types of complications which sometimes occur are given after the different types of operation.

Vacuum aspiration or suction

Vacuum aspiration is the most common form of abortion, with 83 per cent of abortions on women resident in England and Wales being performed by this method in 1995 and a further 9 per cent being performed by this method accompanied by dilation and curettage (D & C) or dilation and evacuation (D & E)[2] (see p 97).

Within the NHS this method is normally only used up to 12 weeks LMP, although in the charitable and private sectors, where doctors are often more skilled because they perform terminations more frequently, it is carried out up to 15 weeks under general anaesthetic. The additional procedure of a D & C or D & E can increase the number of weeks when it can be performed. Vacuum aspiration can be carried out under local or general anaesthetic. The BPAS offers local anaesthetic as an alternative to women less than 12 weeks LMP.

Whether you have an NHS or private abortion you will usually be treated as a day-care case. Admission for day-care cases is generally early in the morning, around 8.30 am, and you can normally expect to be discharged mid-afternoon.

In 1997 the Marie Stopes centres offered a new day-care service which can be completed in a much shorter time. Using local anaesthetic and minimal dilation of the cervix, abortions up to 12 weeks can be carried out within a couple of hours.

Preparation

If you are having the abortion performed under general anaesthetic you will not be allowed to smoke, eat or drink anything (or even chew gum) after midnight of the night before the operation. If you have a heavy cold or temperature you will be unable to have a general anaesthetic as this increases the risk associated with anaesthesia. You may also be asked to have a bath before you go into the theatre or to have one before going to the clinic. You will need to take a nightdress, dressing gown, slippers, sanitary pads, as well as books or magazines.

Prior to going into the operating theatre you will need to put on a hospital gown and, if you have long hair, a hat. You may or may not be given some form of premedication, either in the form of a tablet or injection. This will relax you and make you feel drowsy but if combined with general anaesthetic lengthens the recovery time and is therefore rarely used for day-care abortions.

The operation

The operating procedure is exactly the same whether the abortion is performed under local or general anaesthetic. You will be asked to lie with your legs bent at the knees and vulva, vaginal and cervical areas will be cleansed. The doctor may also carry out a bimanual examination similar to that performed during the consultation to assess the size and position of the uterus. The cervix is then held in place with an instrument called a tenaculum which can give a slight pinching sensation.

If local anaesthetic has been chosen it will be injected at this point. The cervix is then gently dilated in stages until it is wide enough to accept a small cannula with integral curette. While the cervix is being dilated pain, similar to heavy menstrual cramps, may be experienced. The cramping is less severe if the cervix has been dilated before, either during childbirth, miscarriage or previous abortion. Dilation takes about two minutes.

The size of the curette will depend on the stage of the pregnancy but is normally between 8 and 10 mm in diameter, is not flexible and may be metal rather than plastic. It will be attached to a mechanical means of suction since a syringe cannot create a strong enough vacuum at this stage of pregnancy. The tip of the curette is inserted into the uterus through the cervix and the machine is switched on. The foetal material is gently pulled away from the uterine walls, drawn through the curette into the tube and then into a jar attached to the aspirator. This normally takes between two and five minutes.

If the pregnancy is further advanced, and so is being carried out under general anaesthetic, small retained pieces of uterine tissue may need to be removed, either by passing a small metal curette around the uterine walls (D & C) or with a small pair of forceps (D & E).

How we feel

Some of us choose to have a vacuum aspiration abortion carried out under local anaesthetic because we feel more in control of what is happening, while others prefer a general anaesthetic. With a local anaesthetic many women find the presence of a nurse or counsellor helps them to relax and gives them greater confidence.

I had my local anaesthetic termination on the NHS having been referred by my family planning clinic. I found it virtually painless, much less so than either having a coil fitted or even period pains.

Before it started I was given two painkillers with sedative qualities and another painkiller. These promptly sent me to sleep, even though I was very nervous and a bit tearful at the prospect of what was going to happen. About half an hour later I was taken into the operating theatre, gowned up, and covered in green towels, so that I couldn't see below my waist. I was put into stirrups and what was going to happen was explained to me. In the room with me were the doctor and two nurses. The doctor put a speculum in, followed by something which grasped my cervix and I felt it move around a bit. He then said that he was going to give me three local anaesthetic injections into my cervix and that it might hurt a bit. In the end I asked him when he was going to do it, only to be told he had done it.

He then told me that he was going to open my cervix which did hurt a bit, but only enough to make me suck my breath in but not shriek. I have had my cervix dilated before. They then put the cannula in to suck everything out. This felt really strange but didn't hurt at all. It felt a bit like having your abdomen massaged, or bubbling inside, but I didn't have any sensations of being sucked out at all. I hadn't been able to see anything in the suction bottle throughout but at the end one of the green towels covering the tube fell off so I could see a bit of blood. The suction machine made quite a lot of noise, but I had been warned about this. They then took me out of the stirrups and into a room where I rested for about three hours before I went home. The doctor came in to see me before I was allowed to be collected by a friend. I was given cups of tea, and people and nurses called in to see me very often. I have had absolutely no pain and have just stopped bleeding after twenty-four hours.   *Maureen*

When we are very relaxed we experience very little pain and sometimes find that being conscious during the operation helps to clarify our decision.

I felt very little physically, but emotionally I felt the whole thing become clearer and consequently felt both upset and relieved. There was a nurse assigned to hold my hand and speak to me.   *Theresa*

Reactions

Whether the operation is performed under local or general anaesthetic, you may experience cramps for a few hours afterwards as the uterus and cervix contract back to their normal size. The pain can be fairly intense immediately after the operation but is not unbearable and will usually lessen or cease after a few hours. The amount of pain women experience will vary and depends on the stage of the pregnancy and individual pain tolerance. If you have a low tolerance you may need a mild painkiller such as aspirin, paracetamol or codeine until the pain eases off.

Recovering from the anaesthetic

Reactions to a general anaesthetic and recovery times vary enormously. Some women recover very quickly, while others, particularly those who have had premedication, need a much longer time. If your abortion is carried out in an NHS hospital you will probably recover consciousness when you are back in the ward. With day-care centres and clinics, however, you generally regain consciousness in a recovery room where nurses monitor your blood pressure and post-anaesthesia reactions. Regaining consciousness in a strange place, together with the effect of the anaesthetic, can seem unreal.

It took me ages to come round. I remember coming to in the recovery room where there were lots of women lying on beds. I had very painful stomach cramps, much worse than a period, so I let myself lapse back into unconsciousness. Some time later I was aware that someone was being slapped round the face and being told it was time to wake up. It took a bit of time to realise that person was me!   *Liz*

[I had] a pre-med and I was drowsy for about forty-eight hours. I bled, like a normal period. The bleeding was the sign it was all over and with the flow was the flow of relief.   *Patricia*

The emotional relaxation that the anaesthetic causes may mean that we sometimes find ourselves crying when we come round, releasing all the tension that has built up, perhaps unconsciously, over the weeks before.

As I was coming round from the anaesthetic I could hear this dreadful sobbing and crying and then there was a nurse shaking me, telling me to be quiet because it was distressing the other women – it was me crying.
Rachel

When the abortion has been carried out in hospital, you are generally able to spend the remainder of the day resting in bed. With day-care abortions, however, the resting time is much shorter. After an hour or so you are able to get dressed, have a light meal and then spend a few hours sitting quietly in a waiting room before being allowed to go home. With a local anaesthetic recovery and waiting time is even shorter.

Bleeding

The amount of blood we lose following an abortion varies from woman to woman. Bleeding may finish very soon after the abortion, requiring only two or three sanitary towels, carry on for a few days like a normal period, or dribble on for two or three weeks, occasionally running into the first post-abortion period. It should never at any time exceed the amount lost during a period. If heavy loss does occur then you should rest flat on your bed. If this is not sufficient to reduce the bleeding, contact a doctor.

Pain

Sometimes cramp-like pains can persist for a few days after the abortion, particularly when small blood clots are being passed. These should not be severe and any discomfort can be relieved by taking a mild painkiller.

Complications

Although having a termination performed by vacuum aspiration is a very safe operation there is, as with all medical procedures, a slight risk of complications occurring. These are normally infection, retained foetal tissue, perforation, haemorrhage or complications arising from the anaesthetic.

Infections

If you are run down when you have an abortion you will be more prone to developing an infection in the days following the operation. Infections can be caused by the use of instruments which have not been properly sterilised or by retained tissue in the uterus (see below). Having sex, using tampons, bathing or douching too soon after the operation can allow germs to enter the uterus through the vaginal passage before the womb has properly healed.

If you experience nausea, vomiting, abdominal tenderness, sudden or undue abdominal pain, an unusual or odd-smelling discharge, start to run a temperature however slight, or increasingly feel unwell then you should seek medical help immediately. Most infections can be treated very quickly with antibiotics and rest, but if allowed to spread they can cause tubal damage which may result in infertility.

Retained tissue or incomplete abortion

Occasionally not all the uterine material is removed during the abortion. In most cases this is rejected naturally by the womb a few days after the operation but, in some cases, it remains, and may have to be removed by further D & C. The indications that this has happened are the same as those for infection, although persistent heavy bleeding and haemorrhage can also occur.

Unsuccessful abortion

In a very small number of cases vacuum aspiration abortion fails to remove the foetus. There is a higher chance of this happening when the abortion is performed before seven weeks LMP or if you have a Fallopian tube pregnancy. If you continue to experience the symptoms of pregnancy, such as nausea, breast tenderness or frequent urination, you should consult your doctor immediately.

Perforation

Very occasionally a small hole can be made in the uterine wall by the curette or dilator during the operation. This normally heals of its own accord with time. If a larger perforation is made, the amount of pain and bleeding you experience, both during the operation and the recovery time, will alert the doctor to the problem. The damage done to the uterus is repaired through the abdominal wall and, if the blood loss has been excessive, a transfusion will be needed.

Haemorrhage

A haemorrhage can be caused by laceration or perforation of the uterine wall by the instrument used during the operation and may not occur until after you have left the clinic. If you experience heavy bleeding with large clots, you should call a doctor immediately or get a friend to drive you to the nearest hospital.

Anaesthetic complications

Anaesthetic complications are not related to the actual method of abortion, but to the general anaesthetic. If they occur they will be dealt with during the operation.

Physical recovery time

The physical recovery time after a vacuum aspiration abortion is very short. Some women report returning to work the day after the operation and feeling fine. However fit you feel, it is advisable to take it very easy for at least two days, as strenuous activity can cause heavy bleeding.

Early medical abortion

Since 1991 the drug Mifegyne, also called mifepristone or RU 486, has been used to terminate pregnancy in the UK. However in 1995 only 5 per cent of all terminations were carried out using the drug. Mifegyne blocks the hormone which makes the lining of your uterus hold onto the fertilised egg. The lining breaks down and the subsequent bleeding is like a miscarriage. At first Mifegyne was allowed only in the first nine weeks of pregnancy, but since mid-1995 it has been licensed for use between 13 and 20 weeks, and so its usage is expected to increase. This treatment does not require the use of instruments or general anaesthetic. You take three small tablets with a glass of water in the presence of a doctor. You will need to rest in the clinic for a couple of hours to make sure that the tablets are properly absorbed. After two days you return to the clinic and a pessary is placed in your vagina. This helps relax your cervix, and causes contractions like strong period pains. You may have already started to bleed during the two days between your appointments. If not, you will start bleeding after the pessary is in place. You will remain in the day-care unit for up to six hours, and then return for a follow-up appointment about a week later.

Dilation and evacuation

Dilation and evacuation (D & E) is the most favoured technique used for terminating pregnancy between 15 and 20 weeks.

The preparation

You will normally be admitted into hospital the day before and will not be allowed to eat or drink anything after about nine o'clock in the evening. Before you go to sleep, a pessary or gel containing prostaglandins or a catheter may be inserted into the vagina to soften the cervix and make it easier to dilate. The next morning premedication will be given before the general anaesthetic to relax you; this may send you to sleep.

The operation

If you have experienced foetal movements, the doctor may want to inject urea into the amniotic sac before the operation. As this can be done after the general anaesthetic has been administered, you should ask for the injection then, and not while you are conscious, as it can be upsetting. As with vacuum aspiration the cervix is cleansed and then dilated in stages. With a D & E it can be dilated to as much as 20mm. When the opening is large enough, the doctor inserts forceps into the uterus and holds the foetus by the skull, compressing to allow an easy passage through the cervix. The placenta is then removed and a D & C performed to ensure that all the uterine tissue has been removed.

How we feel

After a D & E we can expect to need strong painkilling injections to counteract the pain caused by the uterine contractions, the dilation of the cervix and the soreness of the womb. We may also be given a drug which causes the uterus to contract more quickly and which also lessens the flow of blood. Because the risk of haemorrhaging after a D & E is greater than with vacuum suction, we need to spend at least the night after the operation in hospital.

Physical complications

The potential physical complications related to a D & E are, with the exception of a continuing pregnancy, the same as those described under *Vacuum Aspiration*. With a D & E, however, there is a risk of cervical damage because of the width to which the cervix is dilated, even when prostaglandin pessaries or gels are used. Sometimes a cervix can become 'incompetent' after an abortion, that is, it refuses to stay closed during subsequent pregnancies, leading to miscarriages. It can also become scarred by the dilators which can result in its not dilating normally during childbirth. However cervical damage *is* rare, and as techniques improve, it occurs less and less.

Recovery time

The length of time needed to recover from a D & E depends on your general physical health and the stage of pregnancy when the abortion was performed. It is advisable to take things very gently for a week and to rest for at least two days after the operation.

Prostaglandin or induced abortions

A prostaglandin abortion is the second most common abortion technique in later pregnancy. It is normally used from 15 weeks LMP upwards and causes the foetus to be expelled through induced uterine contractions similar to those which occur in childbirth. The BPAS offers induced medical abortion between 20 and 24 weeks. This method accounted for 1.4 per cent of all abortions performed on women resident in England and Wales in 1995.[3]

Having an abortion by this method is emotionally more stressful than the other techniques described since it involves spending several hours in labour and is very similar to actual childbirth. Because it is performed after you have been pregnant for many weeks you often arrive for the termination feeling exhausted and run down. You may have experienced problems obtaining an abortion and feel let down by, and fearful of, the medical profession. You may have had to cope with learning that the foetus you were carrying was in some way abnormal. You may have gone through the break-up of a relationship and have changed your mind about having a baby, or perhaps you have spent many weeks hoping you are not pregnant and have finally had to accept that you are. If you have experienced foetal movements, you may feel that you are killing something by having a termination.

In addition to your own fears and worries, you also have to cope with the pressure exerted by a society which condemns late abortions and the women who choose to have them, without ever understanding the reasons why they are necessary. All of these factors can make a late abortion far more upsetting than an early one and highlight the importance of having sympathetic treatment. In the charitable and private sectors, women having prostaglandin abortions are normally put in single wards or in wards with other women having abortions. In the NHS, however, women are often placed in general gynaecological wards or, in some instances, in maternity wards. This obviously increases the stigma attached to late abortions and encourages women to feel 'bad' and 'guilty'.

Going into labour can be both frightening and painful, although it is not as painful as actual childbirth. Strong painkillers and tranquillising drugs should be available if you want them to help you through the abortion, and it is advisable to check with the doctor before you go into hospital whether this service will be offered.

Preparation

If you are having an induced abortion you can expect to be in the hospital or clinic for one night before the operation and for two or three nights afterwards. Before the abortion is induced, the doctor should check your past medical history to establish whether you are likely to have an adverse reaction to prostaglandins, since some women are allergic to the drug. An abortion should not be performed by this method if there is a history of convulsions, heart condition, epilepsy or asthma. If you have experienced any of these, the alternative is a D & E or a hysterotomy (see below). Until the prostaglandin is instilled, you are able to eat and drink as usual. After the instillation you will not be able to consume any liquids or solids as a general anaesthetic is administered for the D & C procedure.

The procedure

There are five phases with an induced abortion: the instillation of the prostaglandin; the waiting time; the contractions; the expulsion of the foetus and placenta; the D & C to remove any tissue which may have been left behind.

Instillation

Prostaglandin is usually instilled or given intra-amniotically (through the abdomen). An ultrasound machine may be used to determine the position of the foetus. The area around the abdomen will be cleansed, and a small area anaesthetised. A needle will then be inserted, usually a little below the navel, through the abdominal wall and uterine muscle into the amniotic sac and as much fluid as possible drained out. Hypertonic urea is then injected. This can cause a swelling of the abdominal area and you may feel the foetal movements fall away. It normally takes between five and ten minutes. A very small volume of prostaglandin is then instilled. As labour does not always occur unless a high dosage is administered, a plastic catheter is often left in the uterus so that a second dosage can be given if necessary. The waiting time between instillation, contractions and actual abortion varies from woman to woman and is between 6 and 24 hours. The majority of women expel the foetus within 18 hours.

Waiting

When contractions do not start after a prolonged period then syntocinon is likely to be administered. While you are waiting for the contractions to begin, you may experience side-effects associated with prostaglandin such as nausea or diarrhoea.

Some ward sisters may allow you to have someone with you at this time, during the ensuing contractions and after the expulsion of the foetus, so it is worth enquiring whether this will be possible before being admitted.

Contractions

These will probably start slowly and feel like mild cramps. At a certain point the amniotic sac will burst and you may feel liquid gushing out. At this stage the contractions will become stronger and more painful; painkilling drugs and tranquillisers should be available. It may take several hours for the foetus to be expelled and it can help to use the breathing techniques used in childbirth. Depending on the hospital or nursing home you may or may not have a nurse in attendance during this period.

Expulsion

After several hours of contractions the foetus, and then a few minutes later the placenta, will be expelled. The nursing staff will be in attendance during this period to clear away the uterine contents and to settle you down to rest if the D & C is to be performed the following day. You will probably feel absolutely exhausted and just want to sleep, but you may also be feeling very upset and need to be loved and held by someone that you trust. If the D & C is performed immediately after the expulsion you will be taken to the operating theatre and a general anaesthetic given.

Dilation and curettage

After the abortion you will normally be given a D & C under general anaesthetic to ensure that all the uterine contents have been removed to avoid the risk of infection. The procedure is similar to that described in the section on vacuum suction abortion. Depending on the time of the expulsion and the availability of operating facilities the D & C may be performed shortly after the expulsion or the next day.

How we feel

Because we are conscious during the entire procedure we can experience a wide range of emotions, including regret, relief and fear. If we know what is happening to us at each stage and have attentive nursing staff with us, the experience will be less traumatic.

> [I felt] nervous and alone, even though people were there, because they didn't explain what they were going to do. It was emotionally distressing because I felt the whole time as if I was having a live baby. I

didn't expect it to feel like that. The nurses sat and watched, if you called they said whatever was happening was supposed to.   *Sally*

Complications

If you start to feel waves of nausea, heat, dizziness and backache during instillation you should report this to the doctor immediately so that the procedure can be stopped, as some women are allergic to prostaglandin.

The main risks are a retained placenta and uterine rupture. There is also a greater risk of infection and haemorrhage than with a suction abortion. If the placenta does not detach itself completely, this increases the risk of haemorrhage. If a large piece of the placenta does not come away, it will be removed within two hours of the foetus being expelled under general anaesthetic. As with childbirth, there is also a slight risk of uterine damage.

Physical recovery

Recovery from a prostaglandin abortion is usually quite rapid and you are normally allowed to go home either the evening after the D & C has been performed or the next day. You should not attempt anything strenuous for a least a week after the abortion as this can cause heavy bleeding. During this time you are likely to feel discomfort as the uterus contracts back to size and you may need to take painkillers.

Hysterotomy

A hysterotomy is similar to delivery by Caesarean section and is rarely performed. In 1995 only 38 abortions in total (0.024 per cent) carried out on women resident in England and Wales were performed by this method; all of these were performed in the NHS.[4]

Hysterotomy carries the highest complication and mortality rate of all methods, and a responsible doctor will not perform one unless it is impossible for the termination to be carried out by any other method. It is a major operation involving extensive surgery, a ten-day stay in hospital and leaves a scar on the uterus which can affect subsequent deliveries.

The circumstances which dictate the use of this method are cancer of the cervix, or if massive fibroids or a uterine tumour prevent the use of suction, forceps or prostaglandins. It may also be used if prostaglandins are not feasible due to one of the medical conditions discussed under *Induced abortions*, or if the woman is likely to have an allergic reaction to the prostaglandins. If a doctor recommends this method without one of these factors being present, then a second opinion should be sought.

Hysterotomies can be performed from ten weeks LMP onwards, but are difficult to perform early in pregnancy and are more commonly performed between 16 and 28 weeks LMP. As with a late abortion performed by D & E, the injection of urea should be administered after the general anaesthetic.

The preparation

Before going to the theatre premedication is given and you will be partially shaved.

The operation

Once the general anaesthetic has been administered, the gynaecologist will clean the abdominal area and inject the urea. An incision stretching almost from the top to the bottom of the uterus is made, and the foetus and placenta removed. The incision is then stitched. The operation takes from 30 minutes to one hour.

Complications

As with all abdominal operations there is a risk of haemorrhage both during and after the abortion and a risk of the wound becoming infected. Subsequent deliveries will be treated as if a Caesarean birth has occurred. This does not mean that a future delivery will automatically have to be performed by this method. If there are no pelvic abnormalities and the foetus is a normal shape and in the right position, then most doctors will allow a woman who has had a hysterotomy to go into labour. If there is anything abnormal about a subsequent pregnancy, however, then a Caesarean section will be performed, as a rupture could take place during contractions causing an emergency in which the baby has to be delivered very quickly if it is to survive, and if the mother is to be saved the acute danger of a massive haemorrhage. Very occasionally ruptures can occur during the pregnancy.

Recovery

After a hysterotomy you will normally need to spend ten days in hospital and convalesce for six weeks. The amount of anaesthetic that will have been administered may mean you will feel drowsy for at least two days, and you may experience pain and need strong antibiotics.

I bled profusely due to a placenta reluctant to separate. I had to have two pints of blood transfused in theatre. The wound was painful for several weeks and my urination permanently affected, but not severely so. I had acute pain in the front of my shoulders due to referred pain which is a common feature [with major operations]. I didn't really feel 'compos mentis' for 48 hours but that was OK by me.   *Katie*

Hysterectomy

In very rare cases, and nearly always for medical reasons (such as cancerous growths on the cervix or uterus, excessive fibroids in the uterus or diseases of the Fallopian tubes and ovaries which also require the removal of the uterus), a hysterectomy may have to be performed rather than an abortion. Depending on the reasons for the operation, the hysterectomy may be partial, leaving the cervix, ovaries and Fallopian tubes intact, or total, in which case the cervix and the upper portion of the vagina are also removed. It is not a method of abortion but, if your pregnancy has been the means by which the condition requiring a hysterectomy has been discovered, then the foetus will be removed during the operation. In 1995 only 28 terminations (0.06 per cent of all terminations) involved a hysterectomy.[5]

Coil insertion

It is not advisable, for a number of reasons, to have a coil inserted at the same time as having an abortion performed. Firstly, because the uterus is more tender than normal, a coil can cause a considerable amount of pain for several weeks; secondly, its presence may also prevent any small perforations that may have occurred from healing, and increase the blood loss; and thirdly, the string which leads from the tail of the coil, through the cervix and into the vagina, facilitates the passage of germs into the uterus, thereby increasing the risk of infection.

Sterilisation

As with the insertion of a coil, sterilisation should not be performed at the same time as having an abortion. In *Abortion and Sterilisation*, a paper published in 1981 by the *British Journal of Family Planning*, Wendy Savage pointed out that not only is the mortality rate of combining sterilisation with abortion six times higher than if an abortion is performed alone, but that the incidence of regret is also higher. Her paper revealed that when sterilisation is carried out at the same time as a termination, 10.25 per cent of women experience regret compared to less than one per cent when sterilisation is the only surgical procedure.[6] For some women, the regret is so strong that they will seek to reverse the operation and incur further risk to themselves. It also means that the woman experiences more pain after the termination. Sterilisation is more likely to be combined with an abortion within the NHS. In 1991, for example, five per cent of abortions carried out on women resident in England and Wales were accompanied by sterilisation, compared to only one per cent outside the NHS.[7]

Rhesus factor

Your blood will either be rhesus negative or rhesus positive. If you are rhesus negative, there is a chance that the foetus you are carrying will be rhesus positive, if the father's blood is rhesus positive. When an abortion is performed the rhesus positive blood of the foetus passes to the mother and causes a build-up of antibodies to combat the rhesus positive cells. Although these antibodies do not harm you, they can cause haemolytic (blood) diseases in a rhesus positive foetus in a subsequent pregnancy. To prevent this all rhesus negative women should be given an injection of anti-D immunoglobin after an abortion.

Physical reactions to abortion

After an abortion, no matter how early it is performed, you can expect to experience some changes in your body since it is adapting from being pregnant to not being pregnant. Most of these, such as bleeding and uterine pain, have already been discussed under the specific techniques of abortion, so the reactions listed below are those which are common to most abortions.

Breast tenderness

Breasts normally remain painful and tense for about three days after the abortion and then gradually soften and decrease in size. No specific treatment is needed, but they should be supported with a firm bra; a mild painkiller can be taken to reduce discomfort. If any abnormalities in the breasts develop, such as red, inflamed patches, they should be reported to a doctor immediately.

Nausea

Feelings of nausea normally pass away immediately after the termination. If you continue to feel sick therefore, medical advice should be sought.

Lactation

Lactation (when your breasts start to produce milk) occasionally occurs two or three days after an abortion. It is more likely to happen after a late abortion than an early one, as it is triggered off by the loss of the placenta, although cases where it has happened after first trimester terminations are not unknown. A drug to suppress lactation, such as bromocriptine, is normally given.

Avoiding infection

In order to avoid contracting an infection after an abortion you should not use tampons, have intercourse or go swimming for three weeks after the operation. Some doctors also advise having showers rather than baths during this period. Very occasionally we may develop an infection. This can normally be treated with antibiotics and rest if reported soon enough. The signs that an infection is present are sudden or undue abdominal pain, an unusual or odd-smelling discharge, temperature, nausea and increasing feelings of ill-health. If we do experience these we should not dismiss them or put them down to having had an abortion. If we have the slightest doubt it is always safer to seek medical advice.

Medical check-up

We should always have a medical check-up, either by our own GP or at the organisation through which we obtained an abortion, three weeks after the operation. Even if we want to forget the whole experience and may feel tempted not to go if we are feeling well, it is important that we do, as any infection which may be present can be detected at the check-up. If an infection is left untreated it can lead to pelvic inflammatory disease.

Experiencing the operation

Our experiences of having an abortion are very different. As well as our own fears about the operation, the way we feel about the termination will be influenced by the way we are treated by the medical staff, the technique that is used, the support we get from people who are close to us and our spiritual beliefs.

Before the operation
The night before
Some of us experience a great flood of relief the night before the operation. We know that the fight for a termination is nearly over, that any physical discomfort we may have suffered as a result of being pregnant will soon be past, and that we shall no longer have to question ourselves about the decision.

The night before the abortion was the first night I slept

really well for what seemed like weeks. I knew when I went to bed that by the same time tomorrow it would all be over and done with. I felt so much relief, there would be no more doubts, no more anguish.   *Liz*

Or we may be concerned with the practicalities of having an abortion, such as making sure everything is ready to take into hospital. We worry about how those who are dependent on us, either in the home or at work, are going to cope in our absence.

[I was] anxious to get it all over and done with and concerned about the family in my absence. We had not told the youngsters why I was going in.   *Jean*

The night before I obviously felt apprehensive, but I was more concerned to ensure that I had everything listed to take with me, such as tissues, sanitary towels, etc.   *Vanessa*

Some of us worry about the operation or the general anaesthetic, even though we know that the risk is very slight. Our fear is likely to be stronger if we have never had an operation before, or if we have previously had bad experiences of anaesthetics or hospitals.

[I felt] ghastly, feelings of dread, a quite irrational fear of the actual operation. I hardly slept the night before. I was with my boyfriend and we were both tense and anxious.   *Sheila*

[The night before is] burned on my brain. I felt relieved and triumphant that I'd been 'granted' a medical termination [it was before 1967] but I was really frightened that I would never come out alive. I wasn't afraid of dying so much as afraid my parents would find out. The nursing home was in West Kensington and I remember the smell of blood pervading the place. I was angry that it was all so furtive and seamy, and began to be aware of how much money was made out of women's misery and lack of control.   *Nell*

If we are admitted the night before, we are influenced by the way we are treated by the staff and other patients.

I was in hospital for a full day before the operation. I was nervous, slightly embarrassed, but determined not to expose it. I simply wanted the whole business over with. I had visits from good women friends who encouraged my sense of determination not to let the bastards grind me down! The doctors unfortunately knocked most of my confidence out of me.   *Chris*

Admission

Any operation, however minor, is bound to make us anxious and fearful so it can be a great help to have someone come with us to the hospital or the clinic to give us courage and to handle any administrative procedures, such as paying for the operation. If we are being admitted into hospital we should ask them to come up to the ward with us so that they can help us to settle in. Entering a ward by yourself, particularly a general gynaecological ward, can be an inhibiting experience, especially for women who do not speak English or who have limited mobility. If we do not understand what is going to be done during the operation, or if we do not speak the same language as the medical staff, having someone with us can make all the difference between feeling comfortable and feeling isolated and afraid.

The father drove me to the hospital, I found his presence very supporting as I was quite nervous about the operation. Also I wasn't sure how the nurses and other patients would react towards me.   *Alice*

A close friend came with me who has had a couple of

abortions herself. I found her presence enormously supportive and helpful. In fact she rather guided me through the procedure as a mother with a young child. *Val*

My boyfriend [came with me]. He was very supportive, his strength and love despite the unhappiness and difficulty of the whole situation. He stayed about an hour – he had to leave for a lecture – by then I was prepared for the theatre more or less and felt nothing very much.   *Sheila*

Some hospitals or clinics will allow us to have a friend or relative with us right up to the time we go into the theatre. As different places have different policies we need to establish whether this will be possible before being admitted.

My friend stayed overnight with me in the same room. Her presence was comforting because of all the strange faces encountered and the language block, it was a great relief to have a friend there.   *Marie*

My tutor warden came with me. Her presence was great, as she could explain words and procedures to me in easy words. She stayed until I had to go to bed and then I felt terrible as nearly all the people were foreign.   *Sally*

But the person who comes with us may not always be able to make us feel comfortable. We may feel bad about what we are doing and believe that they feel the same way, or we may feel guilty about asking them to help us.

My mum took me to the clinic and then left – I felt terribly alone when she'd gone but I don't think I could have borne her waiting for me. I felt very weepy. *Rachel*

The sister and brother-in-law of my friend took me to the hospital and loaned me as much money as I needed and I stayed with them before and after the termination. I was very embarrassed by commandeering their time and money for such a thing. I was ashamed. They just dropped me off, I think they offered to come in, but I didn't want them to.   *Nell*

Or occasionally we may ask someone to come with us who is incapable of giving us the support we need.

My boyfriend came because I had to check in at 9 am and had no time to go to the bank, so he had to draw out the cash for me. He seemed to be fairly casual and did not understand how I felt. I did not find his presence a comfort.   *Margo*

The man who made me pregnant took me to the nursing home . . . I thought it was about time he took some responsibility. His presence in the waiting room was an embarrassment, very few of the other women had men with them and those that did were obviously very close to them. I just wanted him to get out.   *Liz*

Waiting for the operation

As with any operation, we may feel tense and scared while we are waiting to be taken down to the theatre for our operation, particularly if the wait is a long one. Some of us, although afraid, manage to keep very calm and controlled at this time.

I felt that this was the time to say 'Stop!', if that was what I wanted, but it wasn't. I also felt that it would have been very easy to become over-emotional psychologically and start thinking things like, 'They are going to take my baby away.'   *Vanessa*

Talking to other women while we are waiting may lessen the tension and make us feel supported by their interest and care. Nurses and doctors who are understanding can also help us to relax.

I was afraid, but somehow calm. The team in the operating theatre were friendly and quite reassuring. I felt as if I was floating just as the anaesthetic began to take effect and then passed out.   *Margo*

I was very calm, all the other women in the ward wished me luck just before I left and the anaesthetist and consultant were great – they told me not to worry as all my troubles would soon be over.   *Alice*

Many of us are understandably frightened by the prospect of an operation which we cannot control. Having to leave our bodies in the hands of the doctors can be quite terrifying.

I was scared. Someone said to me, as the anaesthetic was being given, that it wasn't too late to change my mind and that made me rather distressed and, in retrospect, rather angry – it may have been meant kindly but it didn't help.   *Rachel*

I was very upset and reluctant to put my legs up in the stirrups. I felt like a little girl being punished and wanted comfort from my mother.   *Marie*

If we are not absolutely happy about our decision to have an abortion, or have been pushed into it by others, we may, when faced with the actual operation, feel like leaving. This can be very difficult, as part of us may be telling us that we have no option and that it is too late; we may be afraid to stand up to the medical staff and tell them that we have changed our mind; or we may be worried that if we did leave we would regret it and would be refused a second chance.

Well I think if someone had been there and had said, 'You don't have to go through with this, would you like to go home?', then I would have gone. It was just because everything was rolling I felt quite idiotic. I had misgivings all the time, I had misgivings while I was making up my mind.   *Betty*

I can remember thinking, 'I don't have to do this, it isn't too late, I can just get up and leave.' But then I remembered the recent injection [pre-med] and the previous drug I had taken and worried about foetal damage. If it wasn't for that I think I might very well have left. I felt scared before the general anaesthetic, very scared.   *Cath*

For some of us the whole experience has simply been too much to cope with and we feel exhausted, numb and unreal.

I felt very little. I think by that stage I was so emotionally low that I was close to permitting and consenting to anything.   *Chris*

Because obtaining an abortion can involve confronting the prejudices of others and coping with delays, our main feelings at the point of the operation can be one of relief because we have managed to overcome all the obstacles the system has put in our way.

[I was] relieved at seeing the anaesthetist – he was funny – and I now believed they would do the operation. As the pre-med took effect, the doctor came in for the money which I had to hand over in cash before I lost consciousness. [pre-1967]   *Nell*

After the operation
Not being pregnant
Our first reaction when we realise we are no longer pregnant can be one of immense relief, of having come through an ordeal safely and with the knowledge that

weeks of worry and anxiety are over.

> Relieved and depressed. A bit astounded that the world didn't end and I was not crucified with guilt. Empty.   *Janet*

Our feelings of relief may be mingled with feelings of sadness or depression, we may need to cry in order to mourn what we have lost, or to release the tension that has been building up since we first thought that we were pregnant:

> I felt emotionally tearful, very fragile. Having survived haemorrhaging – a new fresh feeling of having 'just come through' a most frightening ordeal.   *Katie*

For most of us having an abortion will ultimately lead to a greater understanding of ourselves and our needs. Although this generally happens during the weeks and months that follow the operation, some of us do begin to experience a new awareness immediately.

> [I was] depressed and weepy, but very relieved. I was able to get back to living and I was clearer about how I wanted to live and relate sexually to others. *Cheryl*

Attitudes of the medical staff

While we are in the hospital or clinic we are likely to be more than usually sensitive to, and aware of, the attitudes of the medical staff and the other patients with whom we come into contact. Their reactions are all-important in determining how secure we feel at that time and whether we later remember the operation as being a positive or negative experience. We are more likely to be affected by the nurses than we are by the doctors, partly because we have far more contact with them, and partly because we have higher expectations of receiving sympathetic treatment from them as most of them will be women.

The nurses were really nice, very matter-of-fact about shaving me [this is no longer done] and doing all the other awful things but reassuring about the abortion itself. The doctors were also nice, they seemed to be genuinely concerned about the type of contraception I should use in the future.   *Alice*

The friendliest and kindest was the SEN who gave me a pre-med. She smiled and held my hand to the theatre. The anaesthetist was kind and treated me as though I was going to have a operation and not a termination. *Patricia*

Since an abortion, like any other operation, is a surgical process, we should be treated with as much sympathy and care as if we were having a different procedure carried out. Some nurses find abortions upsetting or do not agree with them in principle and therefore treat us with distaste. Being ignored can be as upsetting as being confronted directly with disapproval.

The nurses were offhand and did not explain what would happen. I was left alone all morning in a single room dressed in ridiculous paper clothes and a bath hat! One doctor examined me on the evening of the day I had the termination. She checked me quickly, asked if I had any pain and then left. I discharged myself that same night as I didn't like the clinic. *Margo*

The nurses were cool, naturally, but in a defensive threatened way but also because of my nursing qualifications. When my milk came, three days after the operation, I was distraught and they were nothing like they should have been . . . One male doctor on nights sat for a while while I cried with engorged breasts and aching arms and then drove off in the rain to fetch bromocriptine to suppress lactation . . . The anaesthetist was very understanding and prescribed very effective pre-med and post-operative medication. *Katie*

Often we meet with different reactions from different nurses and having one who is not judgemental can help to break the isolating barriers which others may have created.

Some made their dislike of abortion very apparent. Some were efficient and pleasant. I only remember an older nurse who treated me with kindness. I was in the maternity hospital as the theatres in the general hospital were closed (I think it was the anaesthetists who were on strike). Most of the nurses were pupil midwives and clearly did not want to be involved with abortions.   *Jean*

If you are having an abortion in a specialised abortion clinic, the nurses will have chosen to work in this environment and are therefore unlikely to have these negative attitudes.

Sometimes, while realising the inherent irony, we may find ourselves experiencing feelings of disapproval towards other women having abortions and the staff who are actually assisting in the operation.

The doctors and nurses were very good. I was morally shocked at (a) not being the only pregnant women around and (b) heartily disapproving that doctors and nurses would choose to do this for a living. Hypocritical I know, but obviously some vestiges of my Catholic childhood still remained.   *Val*

Before we leave the hospital or clinic we may be given contraception and information about how to take care of ourselves. Most of us are anxious to be given the latter as we don't often know what to expect in terms of physical reactions to a termination and are worried that we might interpret any symptoms wrongly due to lack of knowledge.

The abortion charities make a point of giving us printed information that we can take away with us and refer to if we are worried at any point. We may also be given antibiotics to counter any risk of infection.

> I was given advice about tampons, intercourse, etc. Bleeding was mentioned and I was asked if my loss was any more than a normal period. I was told that if my bleeding became excessive, to get in touch with my GP or attend the casualty unit of a local hospital. I was also given a card which explained that I had had a termination of pregnancy which I was told to show to the doctor if the circumstances arose. The nursing home telephone was also on the card in case I needed any advice. *Vanessa*

Many hospitals don't have any printed matter relating to after-care and if we are not given any verbal advice we may worry unnecessarily during the following weeks. The apparent lack of concern on the part of the doctors and nursing staff can be upsetting.

> I was not given any advice. I had to arrange my own taxi to the airport, where I was flying back to Orkney. No one even asked me if I felt well enough to travel alone and I felt dreadful, but wanted to get away from the hospital. *Joyce*

> [I was] given no advice at all on how to take care of myself. Yes, I was worried. I had no idea about what symptoms I might develop as a result of the abortion, which were serious and which were not, no advice on how long to wait before having sex again, etc. *Chris*

Our reactions to being prescribed contraception are generally more varied. Some of us feel as if we never want to have sex again and don't want to think about it, others feel they are being reprimanded by having contraception forced on them, while some are reassured by it, seeing it as a sign that everything is getting back to normal.

I was given a white paper bag with three packets of pills. I felt this was indiscreet as only one other girl in the ward was given a 'white paper bag'! I felt that this problem had been caused through not using sensible contraception and being handed pills was almost done to stop me returning in a month or so.   *Patricia*

Other patients

No one talked beforehand afterwards they were equally relieved and friendly, some more reserved than others, but the experience was an equaliser, like all traumatic experiences shared.   *Jennie*

Unless we are given a room to ourselves we find ourselves in the company of other women before and after the operation. Whether we are able to share our experiences with them or feel we should keep to ourselves will depend very much on their attitude to us, how easy we find it to talk to new people generally, whether they are having abortions or other gynaecological treatment, and how much we feel we have in common with them.

Being with a group of women who are open and warm about their own experiences of abortion can make us feel very good. We have the real freedom to say how we feel without being afraid that someone will tell us we are making the wrong decision. Talking to women who have made the same choice as we have can increase our confidence as we know we shall not be treated with censure for what we have done. For some of us it will be the first time we have felt safe enough to talk about how we feel. Even if we don't want to join in, listening to other women sharing their experiences can be supportive.

> I enjoyed being with the other patients. There was a feeling that we had all been through the same experience which united us even though we were different ages, had different backgrounds, some were married and some single. It was a wonderful feeling of togetherness, a great bubble of caring, there was lots of humour. It confirmed my feeling about how strong women are. *Liz*

If we are with a group of women who are sharing their experiences, but from whom we feel separated either by age, background or language, our sense of isolation can be increased rather than banished. Being with women with whom we have something in common, but with whom we cannot communicate, can be very painful, reminding us of other times when we have been an outsider or felt inadequate or unsure of ourselves for being different.

> [The other women] weren't warm or supportive exactly. Easy to talk to but our circumstances were very different. Mostly married women with children, older and very different politically. Mostly local women. I felt a bit of an outsider. *Cath*

> Before the operation there was a tense and impenetrable silence – I think we were all too worried to chat. Afterwards everyone spoke and exchanged experiences. All the other women were older than me, married with other children – therefore I felt very much on my own and couldn't join in. One woman had her husband and tiny baby waiting throughout in the next room and the baby cried all the time and I found this unbearably upsetting. *Rachel*

Nowadays fewer and fewer women are having their abortions in hospitals, with many NHS abortions taking place in clinics. It is therefore rare that we will be placed in a ward where few or no other women are having abortions. If we are placed in the company of women who are having fertility tests, it can make us feel very guilty and uncomfortable.

> Most women on my ward were there for other things, including infertility; one women in bed beside me had an abortion also. We both knew – but had minimal communication. The other patients tried to ignore me – I felt embarrassed at just being there with the two women who were being treated for infertility. *Janice*

> It was a general obstetrics and gynaecological ward so no one knew for sure who was in for what – this was probably intentional so there would be no embarrassments . . . Everyone kept to themselves. *Cheryl*

Being on a gynaecological ward does not necessarily mean we have bad experiences. The other women may be very compassionate and may not resent our fertility or our decision.

> I met two other women having an abortion, both for the first time, therefore we shared the same feelings and immediately got on well together and were supportive of each other. Other women in the ward were having treatment for cancer, D & C and sterilisation. We all related to each other well, no ill-feeling because I was having an abortion.   *Ros*

Sometimes we do not want to talk to other women because we need to sort out our own feelings by ourselves before we can talk about them, or because we still feel too upset to allow strangers to get close to us and are afraid we might break down if they were to show us any kindness.

Some women were quite chatty and some were reserved – actually I was unusually quiet. I felt better that way.   *Theresa*

Visitors

After we have had an abortion we may suddenly fear that we are going to be rejected by those we care about, because we have rejected the foetus inside of us ('While I was waiting for him to pick me up I kept having fantasies that he'd spent the day with another woman': *Liz*). When we are staying in a clinic or hospital overnight or for a few days these feelings of insecurity can become intensified, particularly if the attitude of the staff or other patients has upset us. It can be a great help, therefore, to have visits from people who care about us and who can reassure us that we are still loved and wanted:

[I was visited by] my husband, friends, one friend plus baby (the nurses were horrified) which with my logic to the fore wasn't distressing at the time, my mother, sister, colleagues. They all reacted compassionately (only those who would understand were told in the first place) especially on seeing my anaemic and emaciated state.   *Katie*

My boyfriend was there for me to cry and express my feelings of losing a potential, beautiful baby. Maybe a genius or maybe great like Martin Luther King. *Glynis*

Although we may want the love of the person with whom we became pregnant, when they cannot understand what we have been through, we do not always find their concern as comforting as we had hoped.

Going home

Going home to familiar surroundings marks the end of a stage of one of the most important journeys of our life, a journey that began when we discovered or knew we were pregnant. Our home has been the place where we have had to face up to our unplanned pregnancy, where we decided we wanted a termination, and where we may have confronted ambivalent feelings. Returning can evoke many memories and past feelings and we may need someone with whom we are close to be with us at this time, to look after our physical needs and with whom we can share both our positive and negative feelings.

For some of us returning home is a happy experience. It reconfirms that we are back in the 'real' world, where we have control over what happens to us, and where we are surrounded by familiar faces and routines.

> The 'father' collected me. I can remember I was really pleased to see him. I was desperate to get home and settle back into normal life as quickly as possible. We talked about how I felt.   *Alice*

Trying to feel normal is not the same as actually feeling normal. Some of us try to pretend that we feel as we did before we became pregnant, while feeling different underneath. Often we do this in order to protect ourselves from painful emotions, or to save others from having to see our unhappiness.

Suppressing our feelings, however, only delays the time when we shall have to deal with them.

> My parents collected me – they were gentle and concerned but I was trying to pretend that everything was back to normal. . . . I didn't want to talk about it. *Rachel*

> I pretended everything was fine. Inside the anger crystallised until it became a knife I knew I was going to stick into him at some point. I wasn't going to let him see that he had hurt me, I was invulnerable on the outside.   *Liz*

Our home often has symbolic connections with the womb. It is the place we retreat to, the place we are most ourselves and the place we associate with security and warmth. After an abortion we may just want to close the door and give ourselves time to assimilate how we feel before participating in active life again.

I just wanted to get back to my room in Glasgow. I felt OK. I went to bed, my refuge when depressed. *Lorna*

Normal surroundings have a distancing effect on some of us. They look the same and yet we do not feel the same. There is no sign that anything has altered, yet we know that a lot has happened. Paradoxically, although we may not have acknowledged a relationship to the foetus, we may still experience a sense of loss or numbness when we return home.

I got the bus home. [I felt] unreal, a bit empty and kind of regretful that everything was so ordinary and something shattering had just happened.   *Janet*

I felt nothing I can remember about, except that I *wished* I felt different about it; feeling nothingness meant I was unable to feel relief or joy or grief to express it.   Chris

For some of us, returning home involves re-establishing our relationship with the person with whom we became pregnant. If at all possible we need to create a safe situation where we can both share our feelings about the abortion, listen to each other and try to understand each other's feelings and perspective. With some men, however, this is not possible, since they can neither release their own feelings, nor accept ours. Difficulty in both experiencing and expressing emotions can make it impossible for them to give us the support and love we so desperately need. Some men experience the abortion as a rejection of themselves, or feel guilty that it has happened. Whatever the reason, lack of support at this time is deeply painful.

> I thought he was awful, he came and collected me from the clinic and said, 'I've got to go and see a client', and took me home and dumped me and went out. So of course it was very difficult for me to feel anything but fury and resentment. I mean there was no tenderness, or affection or reassurance.   *Betty*

> I went to bed and my sister-in-law phoned to see how I was. My husband went out with a friend – I have never forgiven him for that and he now realises it was the wrong thing to do.   *Patricia*

It is important to distinguish between anger and hurt experienced because of the reactions of other people and feelings of depression caused by the abortion itself. If we feel distressed, it may be because we feel let down by someone close to us, not because we have done the wrong thing. Many women feel only relief when the abortion is over, and look forward to taking up their lives where they left off.

4
Post-Abortion Feelings –
A New Beginning

Things generally got worse before they got better, but my life improved considerably within six months. *Isobel*

We all wonder how we will feel after an abortion. We ask ourselves and others whether we can expect to feel guilty, sad, regretful or if we will experience a sense of loss. We wonder if our relationship will change, or if we will feel differently about sex and contraception.

A number of surveys have shown that the majority of women do not suffer from any long-term problems relating to abortion; in fact the risk of serious mental illness after abortion is lower than after childbirth.[1] However, as well as a tremendous sense of relief, feelings of guilt, loss or anger are common in the weeks and sometimes months after an abortion.

Reaching the point where we feel at peace with our

decision is a complex and individual process. Having an abortion touches on nearly every part of our lives, and as well as causing new wounds it can re-open old ones. In addition the issues raised for women who very much wanted to have a baby but decided not to continue with the pregnancy because of impairment in the foetus will be different than for women who did not want to continue with the pregnancy. Resolving the issues that are raised will therefore be different for each of us, as will the point at which we feel able to address them. Some of us may be able to feel and express our grief and anger immediately, while others may not be able to contact how they really feel until years later. Some women find that they only start to fully re-experience and release their emotions when they decide that they do not want to have a child, or to have another child.

Whatever our feelings after the abortion, what most surveys ignore is that an abortion can be used to help us discover things about ourselves that we need to change in order to live more complete and more fulfilling lives. Being pregnant without wanting to be often prompts us to start asking questions about the nature of life and death, our fertility, our sexuality, the reality of pregnancy, motherhood and children. It can also change the way we feel about our partners, our friends and our children.

For some women who are mothers, choosing abortion may be a particularly difficult decision after having experienced a full-term pregnancy, childbirth and parenthood. However for others the decision is relatively straightforward. Whatever your reaction, you may find that the experience prompts you to question some basic assumptions in life.

Although it can be frightening to have to acknowledge the need to change, the very fact that we start questioning, or feel that we can no longer carry on as before, holds within it the potential for constructive development, if only we can be kind to ourselves and make the time and space to let old feelings out and welcome new ones in their place.

This can be especially hard to do if we are tormented by feelings of guilt or self-reproach, so it is important that we remember that our reasons for choosing to have an abortion were valid. We owe it to ourselves not to forget that we did the best we possibly could under the circumstances and to remember that our decision was not made lightly, nor was it easy to carry through. We may have had to make a decision contrary to our former beliefs; we certainly have had to go against society's view of what is 'good'. We may have had to cope with hostile reactions and isolation; and we may have gone through an operation too. Having an abortion is not a sign that we are weak, but that we are strong enough to make a difficult decision that does not bring any tangible rewards. If we can hold on to this, then we shall be better able to make positive use of our experience, and are less in danger of having to cope with recurrent feelings of guilt and anger.

General feelings

For some of us, the abortion is the end of our self-doubts, guilt and questioning. Once our physical health has returned to normal, we feel ourselves again and are not troubled by any unsettling thoughts or depression:

> I was completing my college course so was having to make decisions about where to go next. I don't ever recall having any feelings of remorse, regret or any other guilt feelings women are supposed to experience. I was anxious about owing so much money.   *Nell*

Many post-abortion counsellors, however, believe that

a lot of us do experience a sense of loss after an abortion, which we need to acknowledge. This loss needn't necessarily be the loss of the life we were carrying, it can be an echo of other losses in our lives: the death of a parent, or one who left home; the end of an important relationship; the loss of a job; some part or idea we have of ourselves which we need to let go. In order to free ourselves of this feeling of loss we need to be able to recognise it and then go through a period of grief or mourning while we let it pass away from us. Being able to experience this directly is very valuable.

> I cried a good deal, but I felt this to be acceptable and useful. It took about one-and-a-half years to work through the mental and emotional aspects but this progressed naturally and healthily with much listening by my partner.   *Katie*

It can be difficult to recognise whether we have any feeling of loss or not. We can find it hard to come to terms with the fact that we can experience regrets when we wanted to end our pregnancy in the first place, and often don't see the abortion as a symbol of another loss or rejection. We are also reluctant to give space to regretful emotions because we are afraid that it would be admitting that we have made the wrong choice.

> I don't feel I want intercourse as often as I used to. I'm sure this is some subconscious, psychological problem stemming directly from the termination. Perhaps because I had conscious problems afterwards, or perhaps it was that I did not want to admit to having any, I now have a longer-lasting subconscious problem instead.   *Vanessa*

Looking back I think I tried to cut myself off emotionally from what was happening – possibly because I thought that if I let it get through to me I

would have cracked in my resolve to have an abortion
. . . I think that if very close friends had been around
me I would have come to terms with the emotional
side of it all at the time rather than five years later.
Alice

Society's disapproval of abortion also encourages us to
suppress our feelings. Quite apart from the fact that we
all know, work with, or are close to people who we know
would be shocked by hearing that we have chosen to
have an abortion, we all know people who, while willing
to accept it on the surface, simply don't want to get
involved in any deep feelings we may have. Consequently
we create a role for ourselves which makes us socially
acceptable. We keep silent in certain company, edit our
conversation carefully with others, and are very careful
about whom we talk to openly. This role does not just
affect our outward appearance it permeates through to
our inner feelings and inhibits any feelings of loss we may
have.

I felt I mustn't make too much of a fuss and that comes
a lot, I think, because I come from a very working-
class background: 'You've got a problem, you deal
with it and you be quiet and get on with it', and that's
very much how my family are and my parents, they
won't make a fuss.   *Sandra*

Because it is easier for others if we appear to be 'back
to normal', we may try very hard to pretend that we are.
Feelings of euphoria are very common straight after an
abortion and we often throw ourselves into a whirlwind
of activity, honestly believing we are fine, only to discover,
sometimes months or years later, that we were
subconsciously avoiding what were very real issues for us.

I felt relieved and very strong immediately afterwards.
I felt I could do anything. Then I began to feel guilty

because I didn't feel guilty and then rather sad and lonely and depressed.   *Rachel*

It was a confusing time generally, I had just changed jobs and acquired a really good lecturing post with great money. Too much was happening in my life for the abortion and my feelings about it to be given any place of thought or discussion.   *Chris*

Some of us feel depressed and bad about ourselves, often in a general rather than specific way. Perhaps because we have been told we may feel depressed after an abortion, we find it easier to be like this rather than to examine where the root of the depression lies. In reality we are punishing ourselves and need the time and space to work out why we feel as we do.

I felt as if I could do anything and it wouldn't matter. I was depressed at college. Became slightly promiscuous. Went out a lot.   *Janet*

I got depressed – also suicidal – I would be interested to know if this is a usual reaction to a termination. I don't recall ever feeling suicidal before.   *Jean*

If we feel anger after an abortion, we may direct this outwardly: towards our GP, the medical staff, our partner; or turn it in on ourselves. Outward anger is frequently justified in that some of us will have been treated badly and need to express our rage. The longer we keep it inside us, the more destructive it becomes, since it prevents us from letting other, more positive emotions into our lives.

I hadn't felt angry until the last one . . . and I was so pleased I was angry, I loved it. This friend of mine rang me up and said, 'I know this really good homeopathic remedy for anger you could have', and I went, 'I don't want it. I want to be angry, I don't want to be calmed down by anything, thank you very much!', and it really got me through.   *Sandra*

Frequently we turn the anger in on ourselves and cause ourselves to suffer rather than another person. We may recognise it as anger, or it may come out as guilt or feeling generally upset without really knowing why.

Superficially I felt absolutely fine. I cried a bit in the first week after the abortion, though I now perceive this as anger towards my boyfriend rather than tears for the event. In the following months I was weepy and emotional.   *Val*

Emotionally [I was] in a turmoil. I felt terribly guilty, and would often start crying for little or no reason. I had just started a new job which was one I had longed for and would set me on my career, but that made me feel guilty and I wondered if I had been selfish. *Margo*

Expressing our anger, fury and rage will not make us feel better if the real cause of it lies not with the way in which we have been treated, but with some deeper emotion such as previous losses or rejections. These deeper feelings often date back to our childhood and we may need to work on ourselves in depth to discover their roots.

I hated him for years. I used to see him every now and again to let him know how much I loathed and despised him. Once I even used physical violence and I meant to kill him. Yet I never felt any better . . . Eventually I went to a post-abortion group.   *Liz*

Resolving the issues
Our bodies
After an abortion, some of us find the ways in which we view and experience our body, our sexuality and fertility

begin to change. Initially the alterations in our feelings can be uncomfortable to live with. If our pregnancy was not planned, we may become scared of our ability to reproduce, be unable to relax when we have sexual intercourse with a man, or we may want to disown our body because we feel it has betrayed us. Such feelings are potentially more positive than they might first appear, since they are asking us to recognise, sometimes for the first time, that our sexuality and fertility are potent forces in our lives. Once we can accept them as a valuable part of ourselves, rather than viewing them as an 'enemy within', we can start to discover what they really mean for us and begin to express them in more fulfilling ways.

Menstruation

Menstruation can become a more important and welcome part of our lives following an abortion. For centuries women have been taught to fear their periods, to see them as a 'curse', as a sign of uncleanliness and as something which has no acceptable place in the modern world. Consequently we are encouraged to experience them, not as a vital link with the basic and powerful regenerative life force, but as a function beyond our control, a burden that we have to carry and cannot enjoy.

A termination can help us to experience them in a more constructive way. When we bleed our body is telling us that we are not pregnant and, for those of us who do not want to conceive, this proof can fill us with feelings of reassurance and a sense of being in control.

I had always enjoyed menstruating – after the abortion I met my period with a feeling almost of love.   *Nell*

When I get my first period, I feel that phase one of my dealing with it [abortion] is over. Okay, my body has now returned to normal. I've got my period, physically

I'm getting back and I can start working out when my period is due . . . I then get more perspective on it. *Sandra*

Feeling more positive about menstruation can also make it less physically painful. Welcoming our periods emotionally relaxes us physically so we work with our bodies rather than against them.

I'd always hated my periods before having an abortion and afterwards I was surprised to find myself actually liking them, I also found them less painful.   *Liz*

Menstruation is inextricably linked with the concept of womanhood. When we were younger we were taught to see the commencement of our periods as an initiation into the rather frightening and mysterious world inhabited by our mothers and older women. Once we began to bleed we were no longer seen as little girls, yet we were not seen as adults either. The confusion inherent in this apparent contradiction often accompanies us for years and we find ourselves wondering what womanhood really means to us. Being able to accept our menstruation can help us redefine ourselves as adult women.

It was not so much [my attitude] to menstruation that changed, more the whole female cycle and how it was dealt with in the modern day world. I felt bitter for a time that I had not come to terms with my womanhood earlier.   *Theresa*

When we have wanted a child but have been unable to continue with the pregnancy, our menstruation can initially cause us pain as it reminds us of the loss we have suffered. Feelings of sadness experienced at this time can be used as periods of natural and healthy mourning.

[They were] a regular reminder of the termination and I always remembered the idea of menstruation

suggesting the womb weeping, as I usually did.
Katie

Sexuality

Many of us find that having an abortion changes the way we feel about our sexuality. After the abortion we may find that we do not enjoy full intercourse with men as much as we may have done before. We feel tense and nervous, are unable to 'let go', avoid close relationships or do not want to have sex at all. These reactions may be fearful ones and, depending on where our own fears are rooted, will either pass away quite quickly or persist until we are able to understand their basis. Whatever the cause of our changed feelings, it is important to acknowledge them and allow ourselves time to think through what these changed feelings mean. It is important to remember that we have every right not to have sex if we are not interested, regardless of pressure to do so.

> Sexual intercourse really did not interest me for almost six months and caused problems in our lives which took a long time to work through.   *Patricia*

> Initially my libido was very low but after about a year of resentment and cynicism, there was a definite urgency and need for sexual fulfilment.   *Katie*

Very often we become scared of sex because we are worried that we shall become pregnant again and have to have another abortion, or because intercourse reminds us of the experience we have just been through. These feelings of anxiety often decrease as we learn to trust our chosen method of contraception and share our feelings with our partner.

> It really affects my attitude to sex a lot, because all the time there is a threat of being pregnant it completely stops me from having orgasms . . . I know it's daft,

because whether I have an orgasm or not it's not going to affect my fertility . . .   *Sandra*

I felt very strange about the thought of sex – I couldn't detach it from the fear, pain and humiliation I had just experienced. I decided to abstain from sex for a while. *Margo*

Our initial feelings of fear can often uncover other worries we have about the way in which we express our sexuality. We may start to notice that our partner is the more dominant one sexually, that we are rarely the one to instigate sexual activity, or that we are not pleasured in the ways we like. Used constructively these feelings of fear can encourage us to discover what our real needs are.

It took several years, but eventually I had to accept that I needed to take control of my sexual feelings and say what I wanted. You can't go on hoping they're just going to know, that's too passive.   *Liz*

It may be inappropriate to pick out an abortion as a major cause of change in sexual identity and practice, but it feels now as though it was the final straw. I still felt some affection for my husband for a year or so, but didn't have sex with him again.   *Cheryl*

[It] convinced me that sex with men was not worth the trouble considering I much preferred women.   *Ros*

For some of us our fear of sex is deeply rooted in the past: we may have been abused at some point in our lives, or we may have absorbed and internalised our parents' fear of sexuality. Realising that we are blocked from fully understanding and accepting our sexuality provides us with the opportunity to work through our past hurt and start to respect and rejoice in our sexuality.

Some women seek to resolve this by establishing relationships with new partners.

[I was] anxious to be desired and to go to bed with a man. [I was] aware that this haste was not advisable, but the need was very strong. I used condoms. *Isobel*

Contraception

Fear of experiencing another unwanted pregnancy tends to make us much more conscious of the method which we use and some of us will decide to change to a different form. When conception has occurred because we were not practising any particular method, we are often anxious, once we recommence sexual relations with men, to find a form that will suit us.

After the abortion I went straight on to the triphasic pill. I was happy to do this, as I had decided on this before I knew I was pregnant. I am much more careful now, once when I forgot my pills and ovulated and in a foolish moment had intercourse, I went straight to my GP and got the 'morning-after' pill.   *Liz*

Very often the method we choose, or the one that we change to, particularly when we are younger, is an oral contraceptive. This is not only because it is the method which many doctors encourage us to accept, but also because it has a low failure rate and does not require us to anticipate when we want sex, which can increase our anxiety. If we are older we may choose the coil for the same reason. Many women now combine their chosen method of contraception with condoms to reduce the risk of sexually transmitted diseases such as HIV. Feeling safe can help us to overcome our initial worries about another pregnancy and, once we have regained our confidence, we can explore alternatives if we wish.

[I was] still unwilling to take the pill, or have a coil but was resigned to the fact that taking the pill must be preferable to risking another abortion.   *Sheila*

I have since had a coil fitted which is a Godsend. You don't even have to think about precautions and dangers of them, such as the pill, etc.   *Barbara*

If our pregnancy has been due to contraception failure it can take us several months to trust any method of birth control sufficiently to feel relaxed about sexual relations, however low its failure rate. Often we feel angry that we are the ones who ultimately carry the responsibility because only we can become pregnant. We resent whatever form we are using and experience anger at our partners' apparent freedom. Sometimes we can find it helpful if we insist our partner participates in contraception, either by using a condom, checking our cap is in place, or remembering the time we take our pill.

I didn't feel that anything would protect me from pregnancy and became neurotic if I had diarrhoea and vomiting whilst taking the pill.   *Patricia*

I am very unhappy about the emphasis it makes on my sexuality; if I put it [cap] in before it is a very definite statement of my intentions and my demands. If I leave it out until the point before penetration it means I've been careless.   *Chris*

Some of us continue quite happily with the method we were using before our pregnancy because we prefer it to any of the alternatives and realise that, if used conscientiously, it is unlikely to let us down a second time.

It is, of course, imperative that we use a condom or practise safe sex when having intercourse with a new partner, as other methods of contraception do not protect against HIV and other sexually transmitted diseases. The method used is no longer just a matter of preventing pregnancy.

Motherhood

Our abortion can raise a lot of questions relating to motherhood. It can make us assess how much of our identity as a woman is invested in being a mother, it may prompt us to try to find out how much we really want a child, or to have more children, and it can encourage us to find out whether it is a child we need or whether our pregnancy was a symbol of a desire to express our lives in a more creative way.

To begin with we frequently feel confused. We may feel unable to let go of the life we have created and hang on to it by imagining it is still with us. These feelings, although they may appear so at the time, are rarely an indication that we made the wrong decision. More often they represent some part of ourselves that we need, but are unwilling, to let go. This may be an identity we have created for ourselves, an attachment to an old relationship, or an idealised view of motherhood. Finding out what the 'child' symbolises not only frees us from remorse, but also opens up new channels of understanding and action.

> For the first few years after my abortion I imagined celebrating birthdays for my child. The feeling did leave me eventually.   *Marie*

We may experience a strong, or even compulsive, desire to have a child after an abortion. For some of us these feelings will be a genuine sign that we are ready to have a child, particularly if we wanted children before, if we were pressured into the abortion when we really wanted to continue with the pregnancy, or if we have spent time looking forward to, and preparing for, the birth.

For others however the desire is not based on a genuine wish for a child, but on feelings of guilt. We feel that we have 'done wrong' and believe that the only way we can 'make amends' is to have a child. It can take quite some time to realise that what we did was right for us at the time so that we do not need to vindicate our actions, and that when we do have a child, we owe it to ourselves and the baby to see it as a new and wanted life rather than as an atonement for a past action.

> For the past three years [since the abortion] I have obsessively wished for a child. The whole experience of pregnancy has opened up an area of my life I'd never before considered as a content. Rationally I understand this desire to *complete* my unfinished business, but in my less objective states, I can become quite distraught at the phantom swelling of breasts in preparation for a child.   *Chris*

> After the abortion I became pregnant, quite deliberately, out of remorse. I was quite prepared to have a child and said I wanted it. I miscarried. *Betty*

Sometimes our desire is an expression of a wish to live our lives in a more creative way.

> Immediately after the abortion I decided I wanted to have children. It was totally unrealistic at the time, it represented a new way of life. When I eventually got my work sorted out and started to do what I wanted to do, the vision of a happy little unit with 'the right man' disappeared. I am realistic about them now. When I have them it will be because I want to be a mother, not because I don't like who I am or what I'm doing at a particular stage.   *Liz*

When we experience yearnings to have a child it can be difficult to be with other women who do have them. We can find ourselves feeling guilty and inadequate – 'How come they can manage and I can't?' – or envious – 'Why should they have what I wasn't able to?' What we need to remember is that 'they' are not 'us', their circumstances were different from ours. Using other women as role-models only stops us from discovering our own feelings about motherhood.

> I think now the women's movement has got to a point where women are expected to be capable of everything and I think that sort of attitude, 'Now it's possible to have babies *and* have a career *and* be financially independent of men', causes a lot of guilt . . . When I see women on their own with a baby I think, 'How come they thought they could manage and I couldn't?' . . . there was a baby and it was crying and I thought, 'I can't cope with this.' And I had a choice, I thought, 'I'm either going to rush out of this meeting or I'm going to take the bull by the horns,' and I chose that and I went, 'I'll hold it!' and I did and I calmed it down. It was like, 'Mmm, I feel all right, I'm not crying. I don't feel terrible and wish it was mine . . .'
> *Sandra*

> I found if difficult to be around children. It was Christmas and there seemed to be a lot of family/children feeling around.   *Cath*

Experiencing pregnancy when we have not had children before can make us much more aware of the reality of both childbearing and motherhood. For some of us letting go of old images can be painful:

> I felt sad that when I did have a baby it wouldn't be quite the fresh, romantic thing we're all persuaded to believe in – 'Young motherhood, radiant and fresh', etc. – for me it would be the second time and all my family would know and it would take the edge off it.
> *Rachel*

Yet by relinquishing former ideas we give ourselves the freedom to understand what motherhood really means to us. Experiencing pregnancy may take away much of the fear that surrounds it, and we may find that whereas we had previously thought we did not want children we now find that at some point we want to include them in our lives.

> It consolidated my feelings that children should be a chosen entity . . . I am less romantic about children than before.   *Val*

> I realised that I wanted to be a mother, whereas before I hadn't considered it, and consequently started reading about it and taking an interest in motherhood. *Theresa*

For others an abortion leads to the discovery that children are not a necessary and inevitable part of being a woman and that we can live fulfilling lives without being mothers. When we already have children it can confirm our feelings that we neither need nor want a larger family.

Abortion after diagnosis of foetal impairment

For women who have planned and welcomed their pregnancy, a diagnosis of foetal impairment and a subsequent choice of abortion can be especially agonising. Specialised support for women in this situation is provided by the group Support After Termination for Abnormality. See the Resources section for details of how to contact them.

Inner voices

Sometimes our pregnancy is the expression of a deep, unrecognised conflict or need. It was the *result* rather than the *cause* of our problems. Realising what the real problem is often requires help from a therapist or counsellor as its source is so deeply buried that we are largely unaware of it. It may be that becoming pregnant was the only way available to us at the time of getting the attention and love we desperately needed from others. Or it could be that we needed to test the strength of the relationship we were in. Whatever the focus of our problem, its emergence and recognition through an unwanted pregnancy can be a major turning point in our lives.

It was not a conscious decision, but a very definite feeling, 'If I become pregnant, it's okay, I can afford to have an abortion.' I didn't deliberately want to conceive, but there was an angry, reckless carelessness.

In the following months I realised I had conceived with a certain knowledge and with full intention of not giving birth. Looking back on it, it was probably totally connected with my dissatisfaction with my life in two areas: a relationship, which at long distance was unsatisfactory and had been deteriorating; and unhappiness at the lack of progress with work . . .

It did make me realise that although I wanted children I predominantly wanted to go on working and further my work prospects first. Also it sorted out the relationship for a while . . .

I have mostly got over the guilt about engineering it but this was very difficult.   *Jennie*

I hoped my pregnancy would somehow sort my life out, I would have an identity, I would be a mother. The abortion on reflection, *did* sort things out. I had to pull myself together and rely on ME.   *Janet*

I think the pregnancy happened because my subconscious was forcing me to start taking control and responsibility for myself. I only realised this two years later at a post-abortion group. I went to deal with the anger I felt and learnt a lot about never being perceived or being loved as me.

Working through it all is a long process, and it's not

easy, but the rewards are commensurate with the effort. Even if I hadn't become pregnant I don't think issues as strong as that lie dormant for ever, but I'm glad I was given a chance then, rather than later, to start sorting things out. And the abortion is always a signpost. If I find myself wanting to opt out of responsibility, I can look back and see what the consequences are.   *Liz*

It did clarify some things. I knew I definitely wanted a child later. I knew I couldn't rely on my partner and would have to set up the right circumstances for myself. I felt fairly confident that I would become pregnant when I wanted to be.

I don't know how conscious or unconscious it was. I feel guilty about playing about with human life in order to sort myself out. On the other hand it feels like a necessary and inevitable stage or process and so it is pointless to regret it.   *Cath*

The abortion provided a catalyst and it ended a relationship which would have ended anyway, though I didn't see it at the time. I was very angry to have been deceived into believing I was important to him, when it was becoming apparent that I was not.

I feel so much anger that sometimes I don't know where it should go. Through all this questionnaire this is the only section I am finding difficult to answer because of the emotion it causes. I recognise these feelings of anger but find it difficult to resolve them. I have taken steps to seek counselling regarding them.

I don't think the knowledge that I engineered a pregnancy and abortion upsets me, rather it makes me glad to be able to pin it onto something so feasible. *Val*

Post-abortion counselling

Some of us may need to seek help outside our circle of friends and family in order to resolve the conflicts our abortion has either raised or caused for us. The type of help we seek will depend very much on where we feel we can benefit most. Some of us will feel happier with one-to-one counselling. Occasionally our GP can refer us to an NHS counsellor but as their workloads tend to be high we may need to look elsewhere – to the abortion charities, the Brook Advisory Centres, Relate or to therapists. A list of useful contacts is given on p 179. The BPAS offers counselling free to its clients.

Other people

When we have an abortion it tends to affect not only us, but also the people around us, and may alter our relationship with them. Some people show us empathy and support and we become closer to them as a result, but others find it an uncomfortable subject. They may avoid talking about it or even avoid our company because of the painful emotions it brings up for them. This puts us under great pressure to pretend we are feeling fine, even when we may not be.

> I felt very emotional about it – it always made me cry and therefore I only spoke to very close friends when it was really necessary. I felt that no one wanted to hear and that I shouldn't indulge myself by talking about it.   *Rachel*

Our relationship can also alter with people whom we don't tell about our abortion. They think they are close to us and understand us, yet we know there is a part of our life that is hidden from them so we automatically feel distanced.

Our partner

An abortion is often the make or break point in the relationship with the man with whom we became pregnant. When he has supported us, listened to our fears, worries and anger, shared his feelings with us and cared for us afterwards, then a strong bond is formed. We have been through a difficult experience together and our relationship has survived. It gives us a feeling of permanence and security, and lets us know that the relationship is right for us:

> I strongly felt we should break up, but this feeling passed and in a way I feel closer to him than before. *Sheila*

For many women, however, this does not happen. Men are often afraid of our ability to reproduce because it is something they are unable to fully experience and therefore find difficult to understand from our perspective. Just as the abortion raises questions for us about how important the relationship is, so some men find themselves wondering whether they feel enough for us to want to be with us when we do want children. If they decide that they are ready to make an ultimate commitment they may see the abortion in terms of rejection – 'She doesn't really want me because she is aborting our child.'

Sadly most men find it difficult to understand and express their real feelings. Consequently they may misunderstand how they really feel, or deny their emotions completely, shutting us out in the process. If we are feeling vulnerable and emotional we may not be able to help them explore their feelings. Instead we interpret their reactions as a rejection. It may be months or years before they are able to let us know how they felt.

> Although not aware at the time. I believe my boyfriend

was very unhappy about the pregnancy and termination . . . Over the years we have individually nursed our anger and frustration which we felt at the time.   *Chris*

[I was] angry that he had been so insensitive and off-hand about my pregnancy . . . Later on my boyfriend told me his attitude had changed and that he began to have guilt feelings as well, and felt closer to me. *Margo*

I still think it was the right decision but in retrospect it would have been wiser to have discussed the whole situation more fully with my husband and involved him much more.   *Jean*

The abortion may have made us, our partner, or both of us realise that the relationship is not right. These feelings may emerge several months after the operation as we begin to feel stronger and are more able to assess what we want. Any break-up after an abortion is difficult to cope with as it can reinforce feelings of loss, failure and guilt. It is important, therefore, that we get support and love from others to help us through this period.

I think now that abortion is either going to bring you closer together or it's going to break you up and it broke us up. For two months we tried, we really tried. But you just sit in a room and you just destroy each other.   *Sandra*

It can be very hard to let a relationship go, particularly if we hoped that our pregnancy would make our partner love us more. As we feel their love slipping away, our need for it tends to increase, so we try to hold on to them. Frequently we hate ourselves for doing this but are unable to do anything else.

I felt angry towards my boyfriend but I think I

suppressed it. I was disappointed in him, yet more 'clingy' – I think I felt him slipping away.   *Val*

I was horrendous. I developed a relationship with him afterwards, but it was not a sexual one, it was just me going, 'Come on, help me, support me, I'm collapsing on your shoulder.' And he just wasn't interested at all, he just didn't care.   *Sandra*

Whether the relationship ends or continues we often feel a certain amount of anger towards the person with whom we became pregnant, and the less support we have been given the more anger we are likely to experience, particularly if we feel we have been forced into having an abortion against our wishes. It may have taken both of us to cause an unwanted pregnancy but it is the woman who has had to make all the arrangements, take the ultimate responsibility for the decision, and undergo the actual procedure itself. When we feel like this we need to express it in order to free ourselves from carrying the resentment around for years.

I felt angry and very, very resentful towards him – I wanted him to feel something of the pain and anguish that I'd been feeling.   *Rachel*

I felt some resentment at my partner's fitness and lack of physical detriment! This was irrational of course and we both accepted this reaction.   *Katie*

I cut myself off from him mentally, I kind of resented his stability and cock-sureness.   *Janet*

Angry at my lack of power [generally], angry at him putting himself first, his career (he felt) would be affected by my pregnancy.   *Lorna*

Even if the relationship ends we do not automatically leave the negative feelings that we felt towards the man behind. If we have not recognised them, we can find ourselves transferring them to other men until we acknowledge them and deal with them. If we become aware of recurring patterns of anger and feelings of rejection which seem irrational in subsequent relationships, we may need help through counselling.

Our children

Being with our children after an abortion makes some of us feel uneasy. We may start blaming ourselves for not having given them a brother or sister, and we often find ourselves wondering why we couldn't make room in our lives for another child when we have managed it before. If we have told our children about the pregnancy, especially if it was planned, we will have to explain in the most appropriate way why we are no longer pregnant. Some of us will find ourselves becoming much more protective towards the child or children we have got because we are afraid that something will happen to them as a punishment for our decision. If we feel like this we need to remind ourselves that we may not have been happy if we had had another child, and that our unhappiness would have been transmitted to our children, making them suffer in turn.

I still love Rossi and go off into little daydreams about her prospective brother/ sister that *I* got rid of because *I* couldn't cope.   *Janet*

When our children are old enough to understand we may find that telling them can be useful. If we feel they would be too upset by it, or would dislike us as a result of being told, however, there is no point in hurting ourselves further by taking on their distress and anger.

I did subsequently tell all our youngsters separately and they were all concerned and sympathetic and accepting of the situation – one of them said, 'How sensible'.   *Jean*

Friends

After an abortion we need as much support and understanding from our friends as we did while we were making the decision to terminate our pregnancy. The kind of support we need will vary. We may want them to give us advice on how to cope with our feelings, we may just want them near us, or we may need them to sit and listen while we talk about what has happened to us in detail, without giving us their opinion or comments. Often we have to tell our friends what our needs are, since they may be too embarrassed to ask us because they are afraid of hurting us unintentionally. Being able to trust our friends enough to share our experiences can bring us much closer together.

> My friends were magnificent, and would always talk about how I felt if I wanted to. Knowing I could share my feelings helped me build myself back up again. *Liz*

Not all our friends can help us in this way. The picture they have of us may not include that of a woman who has had an unwanted pregnancy, and it may take them some time to adjust their idea of us.

> Some friends did experience difficulty in coming to terms with it once my pregnancy became public knowledge. [But there were] no long-term difficulties. *Isobel*

Or they may not understand how we really feel and assume that we have feelings we do not have at all. This can create a barrier between us which may take time to go away. It can be very frightening to realise that people who we thought instinctively understood us are not as close as we believed, and we may feel isolated, angry and hurt. Often, sharing our true feelings with them can bridge the gap between us, but if we feel our differences are too great, we may start to grow apart.

I was irritated that I got sympathy for an issue which had not really bothered me.

What bothered me was that my boyfriend had let me down and although they didn't know that, I *did*. I genuinely feel that I was expected to be far more traumatised and guilty than I was.   *Val*

I became rather cynical towards some of my friends, attributing superficiality to them. Now I realise it was just that I was changing and they weren't.   *Theresa*

For some of our friends the abortion brings up uncomfortable feelings of their own. It may remind other women of an abortion or miscarriage they have had, of a lost child or a rejection by a lover. It may make them realise that it could happen to them and prompt them to ask questions which they would rather avoid, such as whether they could cope, whether their partner would support them, or whether they want children.

On the other hand, knowing that we have had an abortion can reassure them and banish fears and worries they may have previously experienced when considering the question of abortion.

Friends came to see me and said that in a way they found it comforting because it had always been such a fear for them, getting pregnant, 'Oh my God, the worst thing that can happen', and in actually seeing me pregnant and have an abortion and come out of it took away the fear of it for them.   *Sandra*

When we do not have friends, particularly good female friends, or we cannot tell them because we need to keep the abortion a secret, we can feel very isolated. Coping with our feelings on our own calls for a lot of strength and we may need to look elsewhere for support, perhaps seeking post-abortion counselling from one of the abortion charities. Our experience can highlight our need for female companionship and prompt us to find ways of meeting women whom we can become close to.

> I didn't have many close friends. For a long time it was a real need, I felt very empty, I needed someone to talk to. Now I do and it's very fulfilling. I wasn't close to anyone who knew about my abortion.   *Betty*

Parents

Very often it can be difficult to share our experience with our parents. We are afraid that they would blame themselves – 'Where did we go wrong when we brought her up?' – we are anxious that they would worry for us; we don't want to challenge their moral or religious beliefs; or we are scared they will reject us. So we protect them and sometimes ourselves by keeping silent. For some of us this is easy to cope with; for others, however, it is painful not to be open and honest. It brings back memories from childhood when we have had to keep other things about ourselves secret. Perhaps our parents only loved us when we pretended to be what they wanted us to be, rather than loving us for what we are. We may remember battles in the past when we tried not to feel ashamed of our sexuality, or our ambition, our need to live our life in a way that was different from theirs. Seeing our parents after an abortion can act as a catalyst, bringing these feelings to the surface so that we may find we want to tell them to see if they will accept and love us now, even if they couldn't when we were children.

We can experience this desire either directly or in less easily identifiable forms. The presence of our parents may make us feel guilty, ashamed or generally uncomfortable. If we start to feel like this it can be more helpful to try to understand why, rather than risking being hurt again.

Realising that we are not loved in the way we needed when we were children, or that we hold very different values from those who nurtured us, can initially feel as if we are breaking a bond. In reality, however, we are freeing ourselves from continually being judged by their standards. Accepting our separateness allows us to start rewarding ourselves according to our own values.

> I do not want my parents (aged 60) to find out I have had an abortion. It would very much upset the relationship with them. I had a stillbirth at the end of my 'first' pregnancy, my parents would see it as just retribution for the abortion.   Janice

Even when they know about our abortion it can still be very difficult to be with them. We may feel guilty or nervous that they are judging us and no longer love us in the way that they used to.

> I kept trying to repay them. It was Christmas and I worked like crazy making decorations and tidying and cleaning and clearing the house. I somehow felt 'spoilt' in the eyes of my parents – no longer their innocent little girl.   Rachel

Usually it is our mother we most want to tell. She was the one who gave us our first model of womanhood, motherhood and sexuality. As we have grown older we may have grown away from her, developed a separate existence, even have a family of our own, but many of us will still carry her and her ideas inside us. When we are able to share the experience with her we can become much closer and the relationship takes on a new dimension. By telling her, we are in effect saying, 'We don't have to pretend to be perfect mothers or perfect daughters any longer. We can both admit to doing, or wanting to do, things that as women we are always told we should not.' Breaking the old mother/child relationship can free us from a bond that may well have suffocated and inhibited both of us, and, perhaps for the first time, we are able to be totally honest with one another.

When I eventually told my mother, she didn't react very much, but I have felt much freer to tell her other things now, that previously I felt I needed to keep hidden. I see her more as a friend and less as a mother.   *Liz*

A pregnancy can also bring us closer to her, even if we don't want or need to share the experience. By becoming pregnant we often gain a valuable insight into what it feels like to be a mother and therefore into how she may have felt. This helps us to see her as an individual woman, rather than as 'our mother'.

I became very close, as I now understood *her* lack of control of her fertility and battered body from perpetual pregnancy, (eight [children], seven living). *Nell*

Wanting to tell our mothers and not being able to can be an isolating experience. We can go through a period of being afraid she will find out and therefore reject us. This fear can make us become more dependent on her because we need the reassurance that she does love and approve of us, or it can make us feel estranged and unloved, because we subconsciously believe she does know. Often these feelings pass with time as we get a sense that we need not see ourselves through her eyes for ever.

To some extent I felt there was a dimension in me that my mother hadn't prepared me for, so I felt strange towards her as I hadn't told her what had happened. I really don't know how she would feel, but I probably haven't told her as it would make me look like I have failed.   *Theresa*

5
Repeating the Decision

Repeat abortions are not the consequence of women's psychological maladjustment or negative attitudes toward using contraceptives. The important problem is that health-care personnel involved in providing abortions may find it difficult to accept that a large number of women who are sexually active and who use imperfect birth control techniques can be expected to have repeat abortions. The challenge rests in communicating these findings to those who work with abortion patients so that they may counsel these women with more confidence, knowing that repeat abortion is due more to probability of pregnancy than to psychological problems.[1]

Having an abortion is not easy and no woman who has had one termination wants to experience subsequent unwanted pregnancies or confront the pain and soul-searching that can accompany them. For many of us the fear of conceiving after an abortion is a very real one and we do everything we can to try to prevent it. Yet because contraception can and does fail, and because it is easy to make mistakes, some of us do find ourselves having to cope with deciding whether to continue with future pregnancies.

Just as it is impossible to generalise about how we shall react to our first unwanted pregnancy, so it is impossible to make assumptions about subsequent experiences. Some of us find all or part of the process much easier to cope with; the operation is no longer shrouded in mystery, and we are more confident of our ability to deal with the issues a termination may raise for us. Others, however, find it more traumatic. We blame ourselves for having got into the same position, we are afraid that by having more than one termination we shall increase our chances of becoming infertile. We are frightened by what appears to be our lack of control over our bodies and, for a time, resent our fertility, sexuality and the inadequacy of contraception even more than we did before.

For most of us a repeat pregnancy is not a sign that we have an unidentified psychological problem. It would be harmful, however, not to recognise that a few of us do get into a self-destructive cycle of repeat pregnancies and abortions because we are deeply unhappy. Rather than feeling ashamed of ourselves and perpetuating our punishment we need to treat ourselves kindly and seek help.

Contraception

Becoming pregnant without wanting to on more than one occasion is often the result of living sexually active lives and having no choice but to use contraception that isn't 100 per cent effective. As with our first unwanted pregnancy it is often just bad luck: our contraception fails us, we are not given adequate information about birth control, we can't find a method we are happy with, or we take a risk and get caught out.

> [I became pregnant] three years after [my first abortion]. I was taking the pill. It was safer and it regularised my periods. I was due to go to hospital for a minor operation and was told not to take it. [I became pregnant with] my boyfriend of nearly three years.   *Sally*

> [It was] eight years [between my first and second abortion and I had] one child [in between] in 1982. I was sort of [using contraception]. I think . . . the rhythm method is the only viable [method] along with condoms. It was a miscalculation on my part. *Janet*

Deciding

> My decision was based on career mainly. I felt the situation was the same as before, and having a child at that stage of my life was out of the question. Also I didn't feel involved with the father.   *Margo*

> I was fed up and tired. I didn't want another abortion. The doctor who examined me said the risk was very high that the baby would be abnormal. The decision was easier as the doctors (hospital and GP) determined what would happen to the baby. The main decision was the doctors', but after it had been explained my boyfriend and I agreed. Our views were the same although it hurt.   *Sally*

As well as raising the same issues as our first abortion, deciding to terminate subsequent pregnancies can involve additional factors. If we are still experiencing negative feelings about our first termination, it is all too easy to see our conception as an opportunity that has been given to us so that we can 'make good', or to regard it as some kind of a test imposed on us by an outside force. We may need consciously to separate this pregnancy from the one(s) we have had before in order to make a decision that is right for us. Continuing with the pregnancy because we honestly want a child and are ready to look after one is a positive response. Continuing with the pregnancy because we feel we have to settle a moral score, or pay a debt, is likely to be destructive both for ourselves and for the child.

Several years may separate our pregnancy from our last abortion and, if we are in our mid-thirties and do not already have children, we may have to cope with the fear that this is our last chance, and consider in some depth how much we want children, with whom, and whether we could cope with being a single parent.

'Horror stories' that repeat abortions can cause complications in subsequent pregnancies are common; we are often afraid that we shall become infertile or will later miscarry a wanted pregnancy if we have another termination. As the risk for one abortion, particularly if it is performed in the first few weeks of pregnancy by vacuum suction, is very slight, the likelihood of complications occurring as a result of another abortion remains quite low. The degree of cervical dilation is most likely to be responsible for cervical incompetence, and with vacuum suction this is kept to a minimum.

> It is more difficult because of the long-term effects on my body. Now after four abortions and one miscarriage I feel scared about another pregnancy. Now if I get pregnant I must have it.   *Glynis*

Confiding

If we feel bad about becoming pregnant again we may be reluctant to ask for the help and support we need from others. Often our reluctance is based less on an accurate perception of how our friends will react to us and more on our own negative feelings about ourselves. Since our close women friends normally want to help, it is important that we do not allow these feelings to stop us from trusting them. Withholding our confidence will not only damage us, it will hurt them as well.

> My sister and friends are all close to me. The first couple of times I told them, but after that only my boyfriend. I was embarrassed to tell my friends and sister. The last time I had one by my current boyfriend who I have been with three years. I only told him. *Glynis*

The medical profession

Just as it is impossible to make generalisations about the way each of us will feel about a repeat abortion, so it is impossible to generalise about the way the medical profession will react to us. We may be afraid that our request for an abortion will be met with less understanding and more judgemental attitudes than before, and that we will be viewed as careless or disturbed. Unfortunately these expectations are sometimes confirmed. Sometimes, however, different GPs, hospitals or clinics have a far more sympathetic attitude than the last establishment where we had a termination.

> The doctors were considerate and didn't make me feel guilty, although it was an everyday job they treated me civil. The nurses and canteen staff were all nice and had time for you.   *Sally*

> Three were at a special abortion one-day clinic in Washington, DC and Chicago, one was at an overnight abortion clinic outside London. I don't think it affected their attitude towards me.   *Glynis*

If we were faced with an obstructive GP before or received unsympathetic treatment at an NHS hospital we may, if we can afford it, choose to have our subsequent pregnancy terminated outside the NHS.

Similarly if we are not treated well at a particular clinic we are likely to go elsewhere.

> The doctors were very kind, sympathetic and reassuring. Even the physical examination was carried out with great care and gentleness. Having experienced a less than sympathetic set of people the previous year, I was very relieved and delighted by the second clinic. Everyone I came into contact with did their best to make the whole experience as easy and painless as possible.   *Margo*

Occasionally doctors and counsellors may be unhelpful because it is not our first abortion. We may be refused an NHS abortion on the grounds that we should 'pay for our mistakes', or find that we have been referred to an unsympathetic gynaecologist without being warned.

While some doctors and counsellors are openly judgemental, others can appear to be so by misunderstanding the reasons for our pregnancy. Many people believe that more than one unwanted pregnancy is not the logical outcome of being fertile and heterosexually active, but stems from either a deep desire to have a child, or from psychological or emotional problems. Their discussions with us start from these assumptions and we may find ourselves having to refute the arguments, either that we really do want children or that we are disturbed in some way, before they will agree to a termination.

With subsequent terminations doctors may be more insistent that we use a different form of contraception. Unless they handle the subject sensitively, they may seem judgemental:

> The third [abortion] the woman doctor started to say things like, 'this is your third and don't you think you

should be a bit more careful in future?', and I just said, 'Look don't give me that, because what you see on the paper, there's more to it than that . . . '

I don't like the moral judgement they put on you because it's something you know in the back of your mind and it's such a powerful trick to pull on you. I can just dismiss it, but it still goes in and stays somewhere . . .   *Sandra*

The abortion

Subsequent abortions may be less nerve-wracking than our first experience but our apprehension will be greater if we suffered complications with the last operation or if we were treated badly by the staff.

I was more confident because the doctor advised against having [a baby]. It was easier. The nurses were nice and helpful, they explained everything from beginning to end . . . The doctors were doctors – they did their job – but in a way that didn't make you feel in the way.   *Sally*

I was not as apprehensive as before as I knew the procedures, but as my first experience was not very pleasant, I was still in some dread. The nurses did not know it was my second. They were really very good, explained what could happen and were attentive. *Margo*

Feelings

Resolving the issues raised by a subsequent abortion is not necessarily harder than resolving those raised by our first experience. We may need to confront the same feelings and fears and allow ourselves the same amount of time and space to work through any anxieties we have relating to our fertility, sexual relationships with men and contraception. A subsequent abortion may also be the point at which unresolved issues from the first abortion start to make themselves known.

If the circumstances surrounding the repeat abortion are less traumatic or we receive stronger support from those we care about, feeling at peace with the decision may be easier than it was before.

> I felt great because it was done with 'nice people', in a better place and my boyfriend was there most of the time. Yes, it was the right decision.   *Sally*

Not wanting to have to go through the experience again can make us more anxious to understand our fertility and sexuality so that we can learn to incorporate them positively into our lives.

> In discussing with other women I was surprised at the numbers who had become pregnant after an abortion, often quite soon, like I did. I did consider that it might have been an urge beyond conscious control, but I think it is more likely that a) I felt lightning couldn't strike twice in the same place, etc., etc. and b) I still hadn't come to terms with the fact that I was a fertile woman and could never, never, afford to take a risk. *Margo*

> What really made me decide to have an abortion this time round was that I feel that because my cycle of wanting to get pregnant and having been pregnant for the last two years, that if I'd kept this child I wouldn't have had a choice. There is something bigger than me that is making all this happen and now I do have a choice. But the one thing I can't resolve is the anger at my body . . .   *Sandra*

6
Last Words

Any crisis in our lives has within it the potential for greater self-awareness and growth. An abortion is no exception. As with all crises we experience pain, humiliation, anger and loss. Yet it is by understanding and living through these emotions that we begin to understand ourselves more fully.

Reaching the stage where we can learn from our experience will take a different amount of time for each of us. Some of us may need to revisit our experience a number of times, often spread across a period of years before we feel fully at peace. Like the women who have contributed to this book, we may have just started to examine how we really feel; or we may be working through the issues. Some of us will have already resolved the conflicts and be living more fulfilling lives as a result; while others will be translating their experience into a political or spiritual context, as well as a personal one.

By sharing their own experiences, all the women have offered us strength – the strength to confront our own unhappiness; the strength to make difficult decisions that can open up our lives; the strength to help women who are close to us through the same experience; the strength to identify the social forces which seek to control us; and ultimately, the strength to oppose collectively the hierarchical political, legal, medical and religious institutions that attempt to limit the freedom of women in all areas of life. For this reason, the 'last words' of the women are only final in the sense that they form the end of this book. In every other sense they are a beginning.

I never experienced a moment's doubt that this was the right decision and I can honestly say that I don't regret the experience. My life has been radically altered as I have become publicly identified with the issue and this has implications for every aspect of my life. I don't wish to be self-indulgent about the experience but I do talk to women if it can help them in any way. I have discussed my abortion in the media when it has been politically useful to do so [and] I have spoken at public meetings.   *Isobel*

[Now] I feel stronger and I learnt a lot about how I cope with problems. [It was] the right decision but that doesn't mean I don't sometimes regret and feel sad about it and think about the baby and what might have been.   *Rachel*

I am now much more clear about what I want and when I want it. Ultimately: My Body, My Decision, My Self.   *Val*

[It was] wrong for me. It was against my moral and political beliefs. Sometimes it feels like a dirty secret. I realised my lack of power and control due to the position of black women in society and trying to live up (!) to white 'liberal' mores.   *Lorna*

I think my situation was different to many women,

that I was much more lucky. I want to explain about it all because I think it shows how easy, non-traumatic and positive abortion can be with proper facilities, support, and non-judgement attitudes.   *Ann*

It was most definitely the right thing to do, but I was not prepared for the feelings afterwards, the fact that sexual intercourse became difficult and the feelings of loss and the interest in the date of when the baby would have been due. I feel stronger as a woman and I have learnt a lot about myself. I feel that I am stronger than I thought I was. It sounds trite but I can help people in the same dilemma.   *Patricia*

Since the abortion I have coped better than I imagined I might have. I feel guilty admittedly, but only if I end up never having a child will I truly and totally regret what I did. I still feel ambivalent about it, it was right in the sense of being expedient, but wrong in other ways. I very much want a baby and by my boyfriend, so in that sense I acted against my own desires. *Sheila*

I have since had a baby and kept her, and the overwhelming sense of responsibility that is attached to the rearing of a child was not something I could have given at that time.

I don't see abortion as a gainful experience in any way. In retrospect I have learned more about myself and my developments as a person, but this has been helped very much by the liberation movement in Ireland. And for a woman to learn about herself is to learn about all women.   *Marie*

. . . definitely right, the partnership survived and became much stronger, my career and finances haven't suffered setbacks which an unplanned child would have caused. The personal psychological benefits were useful for myself and also professionally.   *Katie*

I am sure I didn't think I would feel ashamed. Perhaps it was for the best, but I just didn't feel I made the decision myself. I wish now I could have taken more control of the situation and been less dependent on my boyfriend. I suppose having a child in that relationship would not have been a good idea. I feel it was a big turning-point. I developed a more independent attitude, I learnt from the experience to make more of my own feelings and ideas. In fact it even affected me politically and not just women's issues.   *Theresa*

I am more adamant that abortions should be more sympathetically done and more explanations given, and more concerned about the possibility of women having to have illegal abortions. It was very right . . . I have learned that trying to keep everything to myself probably isn't the way to resolve feelings effectively. *Janice*

It was definitely the right decision. Apart from the practical effort of having a child at that point, I didn't feel involved enough with my partner and although I would have bought the child up myself, I would have liked it to know its other parent.

I feel stronger and a bit wiser. I feel much more aware of women's oppression and our general lack of control over our lives. Up till then I hadn't had a direct experience of certain areas of sexism and felt my politics were a bit theoretical.   *Margo*

It was the beginning of my awakening to the fact of women's oppression and their fertility as a tool of that oppression. It was part of the journey. [My decision was] absolutely right. I knew with total certainty that this was what I must do, and never had a moment's doubt.   *Nell*

Chapter Notes

Chapter 1: Discovering You Are Pregnant

1. K M Alcock, 'Teenage pregnancy and sex education', *British Journal of Family Planning* **18** (1992), pp 88–92.
2. D Bromham, 'Are current sources of contraception advice adequate to meet changes in contraception practice?', *British Journal of Family Planning* **19** (1993), pp 179–83
3. A survey carried out by Open Line Counselling, Dublin, 1983
4. M Smith, 'Why Young Women in Dublin Choose Family Planning Centres for their Contraceptive Needs', *British Journal of Family Planning* **22** (1996), pp 145–250
5. Office of Population Censuses and Surveys, Abortion Statistics, England and Wales, 1977, HMSO, London; Office of National Statistics Population and Health Monitor, Government Statistical Service, 22 October 1996

6. A Houghton, 'Knowledge of Contraception in abortion seekers compared with other pregnant and non-pregnant women', *British Journal of Family Planning* 20 (1992), pp 69–72

7. M Smith, 'Why young women in Dublin choose family planning centres for their contraceptive needs', *British Journal of Family Planning* 22 (1996), pp 145–150

8. W Prendiville and M Short, 'A review of family planning in Ireland', *British Journal of Family Planning* 19 (1993), pp 246–7

9. Ibid.

10. I Allen, *Family Planning and Pregnancy Counselling Projects for Young People*, Policy Studies Institute, London, 1991

11. *Open File*, International Planned Parenthood Federation, April 1996, p 11

12. *Abortion Review*, (1997), p 62

13. *British Medical Journal* 312 (1996), pp 83–7 and 88–90

14. J Guillebaud, *The Pill and Other Forms of Hormonal Contraception*, Oxford University Press, 1997

15. Ibid.

16. T Belfields, *FPA Contraceptive Handbook: The essential reference guide for family planning and other health professionals*, FPA, London, 1993

17. Ibid.

18. J Guillebaud, *The Pill and Other Forms of Hormonal Contraception*

Chapter 2: Deciding to Have an Abortion

1. A George and S Randall, 'Late presentation for abortion', *British Journal of Family Planning* 22 (1996) pp 12–15

2. Office for National Statistics, *Abortion Statistics 1995*, Series AB No. 22, Government Statistical Service, 1997

3. Royal College of Obstetricians and Gynaecologists, *National Study of HIV in Pregnancy Newsletter No. 30*, 1996

4. 'Major advances in the treatment of HIV-1 infection', *Drug and Therapeutics Bulletin*, Vol. 35, No. 4, April 1997

5. Positively Women, *Women Like Us: Positively Women's survey on the needs and experiences of HIV positive women*, 1996

6. S Sheldon, *Beyond Control: Medical Power and Abortion Law*, Pluto Press, London, 1997

7. Office for National Statistics, Population and Health Monitor, AB 96/5. Government Statistical Office, 22 October 1996

8. Irish Act p 55

9. Office for National Statistics, Population and Health Monitor, AB 96/6 Government Statistical Office, 29 October 1996

10. Information and Statistics Division, Health Briefing No. 95/23, Scottish Home and Health Department, October 1995

11. Office for National Statistics, Population and Health Monitor, AB 96/6. Government Statistical Office, 29 October 1996

12. Royal College of Obstetricians and Gynaecologists, *Late Abortions in England and Wales*, London, 1984.

13. Birth Control Trust, *Annual Report 1995–96*, p 6

14. Women's Reproductive Rights Campaign London Survey, 'Abortion Services in London', 1984

15. W Savage, 'Abortion in the NHS: Background to Current Practice 2', *The Diplomate 2* (1995), pp 101–5

Chapter 3: Having an Abortion

1. W Savage, 'Abortion in the NHS: Background to Current Practice 2', *The Diplomate* **2** (1995), pp 101–5
2. Office for National Statistics, Abortion Statistics England & Wales Series AB No. 22, Government Statistical Services, 1995
3. Ibid.
4. Ibid.
5. Ibid.
6. W Savage, 'Abortion and Sterilisation – Should the Operations be Combined?' *British Journal of Family Planning*, Vol. 7, 1981
7. W Savage, 'Abortion in the NHS, op. cit.

Chapter 4: Post-Abortion Feelings

1. A C Gilchrist, *et al.*, 'Termination of Pregnancy and Psychiatric Morbidity', *The British Journal of Psychiatry* **167** (1995), pp 243–8

Chapter 5: Respecting the Decision

1. Charlene Berger *et al.*, 'Repeat Abortion: Is It a Problem?' in *Family Planning Perspectives*, Vol. 16, No. 3. March / April, 1984

Resources List

All costs quoted in this section were correct at the time of going to press, but should be checked for possible increases.

British Pregnancy Advisory Service (BPAS)

The British Pregnancy Advisory Service is a registered charity, which has been approved by the Department of Health to act as a pregnancy advisory bureau. Additional services include sterilisation, vasectomy and dealing with problems of infertility. BPAS makes an effort to counsel women in their own language whenever possible.

Costs

Pregnancy Testing: £10
Urine tests will be carried out 6 or more days after a missed period, with a repeat test carried out if a negative test is received. Tests are performed immediately and you are given the results straight away.

Morning-after Contraceptive Pill:
£20–£30 including follow-up.

IUD insertion:
£30 including follow-up and continuing contraceptive care for 1 year.

Abortion:
assessment plus operation £270–£545.

Assessment:
£45 including counselling, medical examination, contraceptive advice and post-operative care.

Surgical operation:
(local or general anaesthetic)
Up to and including 14 weeks day care £225; up to and including 14 weeks overnight £265; 15–19 weeks inclusive £350; 20–24 weeks inclusive £500.

Medical abortion:
Up to 9 weeks £245; 15–19 weeks £350; 20–24 weeks £550.

Counselling:
Post abortion counselling is free to BPAS clients, otherwise there is a fee of £35.

Addresses and telephone numbers

Head Office:
Austy Manor, Wootton Wawen, Solihull, West Midlands, B95 6BX. Tel: 01564 793225

The BPAS has branches and clinics throughout the country. To find the branch nearest you, telephone their action line 0345 304030 for the cost of a local call.

Marie Stopes International

Marie Stopes International is a registered charity for people of all ages who are looking for expert and sympathetic advice on all aspects of contraception, on unwanted pregnancy and on physical or emotional problems which may be sexually based. It provides a relaxed, informal and confidential service and will refer women seeking abortions to its own nursing home or to approved clinics. It has centres in London, Leeds, Manchester and Essex.

Costs

All Marie Stopes centres provide immediate on-site pregnancy tests from the first day of a missed period. No appointment is necessary. Pregnancy tests cost £12.

IUD insertion:
Initial screening, fitting and follow-up visit £110.

Consultation:
30 mins £50; 20 mins £35; 10 mins £20.

Abortion:
Initial counselling and examination £45; medical & surgical abortion from £285; post-abortion counselling from £25.
Marie Stopes International has one free phone number for all abortion enquires: 0800 716390.

Other Department of Health approved pregnancy advice bureaux

The organisations listed below have been registered as approved pregnancy advice bureaux by the Department of Health. They have all been inspected and the charges made to patients and the arrangements made for the reception, counselling and medical assessment of women seeking termination have been checked. This list was correct at 20 August 1997.

While most of these organisations are concerned with the termination of pregnancy, many of them do, in addition, offer advisory and counselling services, particularly on contraception.

Cheshire
Choice Clinic, Park Manor, Knutsford Road, Warrington WA4 1DQ.
Choice, 134 Newport Street, Bolton BL3 6AB.
Pregnancy Advisory Service, 93 Abingdon Street, Blackpool EY1 1PP.

London
Capital Clinic, 21 Glengall Road, London SE15 6NJ.
Regents Park Clinic, 184 Gloucester Place, London NW1 6D5.

Manchester
Pregnancy Advisory Service, 43–45 Piccadilly, Manchester M1 2AP.
South Manchester Pregnancy Advice Services, 136 Chester Road, Hazel Grove, Manchester.

Nottinghamshire
East Midlands Pregnancy Advisory Service, 493 Mansfield Road, Nottingham.

Staffordshire
Pregnancy Advisory Service, 1a George Street, Newcastle-under-Lyme, Staffs ST5 1JX.

West Midlands
Pregnancy Advisory Service, 19/21 Queen Street, Wolverhampton WV1 3JW.
Calthorpe Clinic, 4 Arthur Road, Edgbaston, Birmingham B15 2UL.

Brook Advisory Centres

Brook Centres offer free contraceptive advice and supplies to young people. There are now 20 centres throughout the country, as well as 13 in London, many of which are open not only during weekdays but on some evenings and Saturdays. They offer pregnancy testing, morning-after contraception, contraceptive advice and supplies, and pregnancy counselling to all women. They will always try to refer women for NHS abortions if possible. When this is not possible they refer women to the BPAS.

Anyone under 18 receives a completely free service. Clients over 18 are asked to pay a contribution of £6 per year if aged between 18 and 20 inclusive, or £35 per year or £14 per visit if aged 21 to 30 inclusive.

Addresses and telephone numbers

Brook National Office, Brook Advisory Centres, 165 Grays Inn Road, London WC1X 8UD.
Telephone: 0171 713 9000

Belfast
Belfast Brook Centre, 29a North Street, Belfast BT1 1NA.
Telephone: 01232 328866

Birkenhead
Wirral Brook Centre, 14 Whetstone Lane, Charing Cross, Birkenhead, Merseyside L41 2QR.
Telephone: 0151 670 0177

Birmingham
Edgbaston Brook Centre, 9 York Road, Edgbaston, Birmingham B16 9HX.
Telephone: 0121 455 0491

Brook City Centre, 12-22 Albert Street, Birmingham B4 7UD. Telephone: 0121 643 5341

Handsworth Brook Centre, 102 Hamstead Road, Handsworth, Birmingham B19 1DG.
Telephone: 0121 554 7553

Saltley Brook Centre, 3 Washwood Heath Road, Saltley, Birmingham B8 1SH. Telephone: 0121 328 4544

(Saltley Routes Outreach Project
Telephone: 0121 327 9650)

Blackburn
Blackburn Brook Centre, 54–56 Darwen Street, Blackburn BB2 2BL. Telephone: 01254 692546

Bristol
Avon Brook Centre, 1 Unity Street, Bristol BS1 5AH. Telephone: 01179 290090

Burnley
North East Lancs Brook Centre, Top Floor, 79 Church Street, Burnley BB11 2RS. Telephone: 01282 416596

Eccles
Salford Brook Centre, 55 Regent Street, Eccles, Manchester M30 0BP. Telephone: 0161 707 9550

Edinburgh
Lothian Brook Centre, 2 Lower Gilmore Place (office), 50 Gilmore Place (centre), Edinburgh EH3 9NY.
Telephone: 0131 229 3596

Inverness
Highland Brook Centre, 77 Church Street, Inverness IV1 1ES. Telephone: 01463 242434

Liverpool
Merseyside Brook Centre, 104 Bold Street, Liverpool L1 4HY. Telephone: 0151 709 4558

Manchester
Manchester Brook Centre, Faulkner House, Faulkner Street, Manchester M1 4DY. Telephone: 0161 237 3001

Milton Keynes
Milton Keynes Brook Centre, Acorn House, 355 Midsummer Boulevard, Central Milton Keynes MK9 3HP Telephone: 01908 669215

Oldham
West Pennine Brook Centre, 8 Manchester Chambers, Manchester Street, Oldham OL8 1LF.
Telephone: 0161 627 0200

Redruth
Cornwall Brook Centre, 60 Station Road, Pool, Redruth, Cornwall TR15 3QG. Telephone: 01209 710088

Sandwell
Sandwell Brook Centre, Toll End Youth Centre, Toll End Road, Tipton, West Midlands DY4 0HP.
Telephone: 0121 557 1937

St Helier
Jersey Brook Centre, Axminster House, Devonshire Place, St Helier JE2 3RD. Telephone: 01534 507981

Telford
Shropshire Brook Centre, 14–15 Deercote, Hollinswood, Telford TF3 2BH. Telephone: 01952 200070

London
North of the river: 0171 580 2991
South of the river: 0171 703 9660

Family Planning Association

The FPA is a voluntary organisation whose aim is to advance the sexual health and reproductive rights and choices of all people throughout the UK.

Enquiries about family planning, contraception and sexual health can be answered through a confidential telephone helpline run by the FPA's Contraceptive Education Service which also holds details of local family planning clinics. Leaflets on methods of contraception and sexual health are available (single copies free to enquirers). A wide range of publications are available from the Healthwise mail order service (catalogue and list of leaflets available on request).

Address
2–12 Pentonville Road, London N1 9FP

Telephone Numbers
0171–837 5432 (switchboard)
0171–837 4044 (helpline, Mon–Fri 9.00 am–7.00 pm)

Other offices
Wales: 01222–342766
N Ireland: 01232–325488
Scotland: 0141–576 5088

Republic of Ireland
Dublin Well Woman Centres

Dublin Well Woman Centres provide counselling to women in a non-judgemental environment. All options available to a pregnant woman are discussed in a non-directive way. Addresses of abortion clinics in the UK can also be provided. Pregnancy counselling and post-termination counselling are available free of charge.

Addresses and telephone numbers

73 Lower Leeson Street, Dublin 2.
Telephone: 01-6610083/01-6610086
Counselling Line: 01-6612738

Liffey Street, Dublin 1.
Telephone: 01-8728095

67 Pembroke Road, Dublin 4.
Telephone: 01-6609860

78–79 Lower George's Street, Dunlaoghaire, Co. Dublin.
Telephone: 01-2841666

15 Church Street, Athlone, Co Westmeath.
Telephone: 0902-73550

The Well Woman also runs a premium Helpline – 1550 255255, staffed by qualified nurses/counsellors. This service aims to provide answers to queries that women have relating to their health and will advise them where to go if necessary. The service operates Monday to Friday 10 am to 5 pm. Calls cost 58p per minute.

Other Useful Addresses

Irish Women's Support Group

c/o Women's Health, 52 Featherstone Street, London EC1Y 8RT. Telephone: 0171 251 6580
   This group is made up of Irish women who live in London and who offer emotional and practical support to women who come from Ireland to England for an abortion. They will sometimes meet women at the airport, train or bus station, provide overnight accommodation if needed, and accompany the women to

the clinic. They try to provide financial support in emergencies.

Heathrow Travel Care

Room 1308, Queen's Building, Heathrow Airport, Hounslow. Telephone: 0181 745 7495

Heathrow Travel Care is a registered charity which provides information and counselling to anyone who is using the facilities at Heathrow Airport. It will help women who have unwanted pregnancies. Ask for Heathrow Travel Care at any information desk in any terminal.

Northern Ireland

Ulster Pregnancy Advisory Association Limited

The Ulster Pregnancy Advisory Association (formerly the Ulster Pregnancy Information Service) is a registered charity which has been set up to provide information for doctors, social workers and the general public and to give support and guidance to individual women with unwanted pregnancies. It sees women by appointment, gives advice on what an abortion involves, discusses contraception and abortion after-care, arranges an assessment under the 1967 Act and books a provisional bed with either the Marie Stopes clinics in London or with an approved private clinic.

Address and telephone number

Ulster Pregnancy Advisory Association Limited, 719a Lisburn Road, Belfast BT9 7GU.
Telephone: Belfast 381345

Belfast Family Planning Association

In addition to offering advice on contraception to women, the Belfast Family Planning Association also gives information on abortion.

Address and telephone number
Family Planning Association, 113 University Street, Belfast BT7 1HP. Telephone: Belfast 325488

Other Useful Organisations

Abortion Law Reform Association, 11–13 Charlotte Street, London W1P 1HD. Telephone: 0171 637 7264

Birth Control Trust, 16 Mortimer Street, London W1N 7RD. Telephone: 0171 580 9360
Website: www.easynet.co.uk/bct
e-mail: bct@birthcontroltrust.org.uk

National Abortion Campaign, The Print House, 18 Ashwin Street, London E8 3DL.
Telephone: 0171 923 4976

Pro-Choice Alliance, 11-13 Charlotte Street, London W1P 1HD. Telephone: 0171 636 4619

Women's Health, 52 Featherstone Street, London EC1Y 8RT. Telephone: 0171 251 6580

Positively Women, 347–349 City Road, London EC1V 1LR. Telephone: 0171 713 0222

Women's HIV/AIDS Network, Scotland, 13a Great King Street, Edinburgh EH3 6QW

Support after Termination for Abnormality, 73–75
Charlotte Street, London W1P 1LB.
Telephone: 0171 631 0285

National Association of Natural Family Planning
Teachers of England & Wales, Brampton House, The
Hospital of St John & St Elizabeth, 60 Grove End Road,
London NW8 9NH.

Australia and New Zealand

Australia

Abortion law falls within the jurisdiction of the various
state and territory governments. For details of the
abortion facilities nearest you, contact the women's
information service in your state, or look in the
telephone book for the number of the nearest Family
Planning Association Office.

ACT
Women's Information Referral Centre, Level 1, Block A,
Callam Offices, Woden, PO Box 1074, Woden ACT
2606. Telephone: (06) 205 1076

NSW
Women's Information and Referral Service, Department
for Women, Level 11, 100 William Street,
Woolloomooloo, NSW 2011.
Telephone: 1800 817 227 or (02) 9334 1047

NT
Women's Information Network PO Box 40596,
Casuarina NT 0811. Telephone: (08) 8922 7276

QLD
Women's Infolink Ground Floor, 56 Mary Street,
Brisbane, PO Box 316, Brisbane QLD 4002.
Telephone: 1800 677 577 or (07) 3224 2211

SA

Women's Information Service, 122 Kintore Avenue, Adelaide SA 5000.
Telephone: 1800 188 158 or (08) 8207 7677

TAS

Information and Referral Service Office of the Status of Women, Franklins Square, cnr Murray & Macquarie Streets, Hobart. GPO Box 1854, Hobart TAS 7001.
Telephone: 1800 001 377 or (03) 6233 2208

VIC

Women's Information and Referral Exchange, First Floor, Ross House, 247 Flinders Street, Melbourne VIC 3000.
Telephone: 1800 136 570 or (03) 9654 6844

WA

Women's Information Service, Women's Policy Development Office, First Floor, West Australia Square, 141 St George's Terrace, Perth WA 6000.
Telephone: 1800 199 174 or (09) 264 1900

New Zealand

The Contraception, Sterilisation and Abortion Act 1977 permits abortion in certain circumstances. The main conditions are that continuing the pregnancy would result in serious danger (not being danger normally associated with childbirth) to the life, or to the physical or mental health of the woman or girl; or that there is a substantial risk that the child, if born, would be seriously handicapped. There is no upper limit for the carrying out of abortions, but stricter conditions apply after 20 weeks' gestation.

A three-person committee, the Abortion Supervisory Committee, licenses institutions where abortions are performed and appoints certifying consultants to consider cases. An abortion is authorised if two certifying consultants agree that the provisions of the law are met.

Abortion Counselling

The Family Planning Association (FPA) works to promote a positive view of sexuality and to enable people to make informed choices about their sexual and reproductive health. They provide unbiased counselling in sexuality, fertility and relationship issues, including unplanned pregnancy and abortion.

There are FPA clinics throughout New Zealand. To find the one nearest you, contact your regional office.

Northern Regional Office and Educational Unit, 2nd Floor, 30 Ponsonby Road, PO Box 68–245, Newton, Auckland. Telephone: 9 360 0360

Central Regional Office and Education Unit, Margaret Sparrow Centre, 7th Floor, 35–37 Victoria Street, PO Box 24–064, Wellington. Telephone: 4 499 2036

Southern Regional Office and Education Unit, Montreal Street Centre, Arts Centre, 301 Montreal Street, PO Box 2137, Christchurch. Telephone: 3 379 0514

Te Puawai Tapu is the parallel Maori organisation to the Family Planning Association. It can be contacted at PO Box 6044, Te Aro, Wellington. Telephone: 4 801 8859

Further Reading

J Hadley, *Abortion: Between Freedom and Necessity*, Virago, London 1996

D Haslam, *Coping with a Termination: Advice on the emotional and practical difficulties of an unwanted pregnancy*, Cedar, London, 1996

S Sheldon, *Beyond Control: Medical power and abortion law*, Pluto Press, London, 1997

Jenny Morris, *Pride Against Predjudice: Transforming*

Attitudes to Disability, The Women's Press, London 1991
——(ed) *Encounters with Strangers: Feminism and Disability*, The Women's Press, London 1996

The Women's Press Handbook Series

Valerie Hey, Catherine Itzin, Lesley Saunders and
Mary Anne Speakman, Editors
Hidden Loss
Miscarriage and Ectopic Pregnancy

Second Edition – Fully revised and updated

Why is the reality of a pre-birth loss so often hidden by
euphemisms or evasions? Why can it be so difficult for us to
grieve over a miscarriage or ectopic pregnancy?

One in five pregnancies fail – yet miscarriage remains a footnote
in most pregnancy books, its emotional and physical impact
minimised. Now, this vitally important and urgently needed
handbook draws on women's personal accounts to fully explore
the experience of pre-birth loss. Finally recognising miscarriage
and ectopic pregnancy as bereavements, *Hidden Loss* offers a
thorough understanding of the experience of mourning, discusses
self-help techniques to aid the healing process, and provides
essential information about the known causes of pre-birth loss as
well as about GPs and hospital practices.

Health/Women's Studies £7.99
ISBN 0 7043 4457 2

Stephanie Dowrick
Intimacy and Solitude
Balancing Closeness and Independence

Why is it that when we are in intimate relationships, we may often feel dissatisfied, inadequate and claustrophobic? But then, once we are on our own, we get lonely and have difficulties enjoying solitude? In this internationally bestselling book, Stephanie Dowrick draws on a wide range of personal experiences, and on psychotherapy's most useful insights, to show how success in intimacy depends on success in solitude — and vice versa.

Further, we have to discover, be comfortable with, like and accept our *selves* in order to know, love and accept other people in all their complexity. A warm, indispensable work, *Intimacy and Solitude* enables us to discover our own unique inner world, and offers real possibilities for lasting change.

'Sympathetically, and with a rare clarity, it offers penetrating insights into some of the most basic paradoxes of human relationships.' *Guardian*

'Essential reading ...A penetrating, thoroughly researched, thoughtful and thought-provoking analysis. Don't stay home on your own without it.'
Mary Scott, *Everywoman*

Self-help/Therapy/Sexual Politics £7.99
ISBN 0 7043 4308 8